PAULA DEEN'S
COOKBOOK FOR
THE Lunch-Box SET

PAULA DEEN

with Martha Nesbit
Illustrated by Susan Mitchell

Simon & Schuster Books for Young Readers
New York London Toronto Sydney

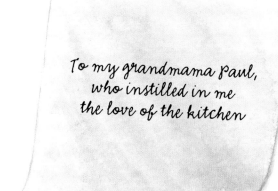

To my grandmama Paul,
who instilled in me
the love of the kitchen

SIMON & SCHUSTER BOOKS FOR YOUNG READERS
An imprint of Simon & Schuster Children's Publishing Division
1230 Avenue of the Americas, New York, New York 10020
Copyright © 2009 by Paula Deen
All rights reserved, including the right of reproduction in whole or in part in any form.
SIMON & SCHUSTER BOOKS FOR YOUNG READERS is a trademark of Simon & Schuster, Inc.
For information about special discounts for bulk purchases, please contact Simon & Schuster Special
Sales at 1-866-506-1949 or business@simonandschuster.com.
The Simon & Schuster Speakers Bureau can bring authors to your live event. For more information
or to book an event, contact the Simon & Schuster Speakers Bureau at 1-866-248-3049 or visit our
website at www.simonspeakers.com.
Book design by Alicia Mikles
The text for this book is set in Neutraface and Pike.
The illustrations for this book are rendered in acrylic.
Manufactured in China
10 9 8 7 6 5 4 3 2 1
Library of Congress Cataloging-in-Publication Data
Deen, Paula H., 1947–
Paula Deen's cookbook for the lunch-box set / Paula Deen with Martha Nesbit ; illustrated by Susan
Mitchell. — 1st ed.
p. cm. — (Simon & Schuster books for young readers)
ISBN 978-1-4169-8268-5
1. Cookery—Juvenile literature. 2. Lunchbox cookery—Juvenile literature. I. Mitchell, Susan K. II. Title.
III. Title: Cookbook for the lunch-box set.
TX652.5.D437 2009
641.5'123—dc22
2009008567

A special thank-you to Ms. Grace/Merritt Model Management, Savannah, Georgia,
for providing the sweet children on the cover of this book.

Acknowledgments

Thanks to Martha Nesbit and Cheryl Jay's Oglethorpe Charter School Cooking Club, who told me what they like to eat! Also, thanks to the Simon & Schuster Books for Young Readers team—Emily Meehan, Courtney Bongiolatti, Justin Chanda, Dorothy Gribbin, Lucy Ruth Cummins, Lisa Ford, Erica Stahler, and Alicia Mikles.

When _Paula Deen's My First Cookbook_ came out in October of 2008, I was thrilled to see all of the young fans who came to my cookbook signings. I just loved meeting all you precious little people!

Now it's time for the next step. The recipes in this cookbook will help you grow as a cook. Cooking is also a wonderful way to bond with people. It was the way I bonded with my grandmother Hiers, my grandmother Paul, my aunt Peggy, my aunt Trina, and my sons, Jamie and Bobby. I am loving every minute bonding in the kitchen with my grandson, Jack. I want you to develop the kind of memories I have, cooking with the people you love the most.

As I said in _My First Cookbook_, I believe that cooking is not only for memory making, but that it is also a creative outlet, a way for you to express yourself to your friends and family. I've always found that cooking is therapeutic. If something is bothering you, you can get into the kitchen and not think about anything that is worrying you. Sometimes, at your age, it feels as if the world is topsy-turvy. Cooking can make you feel much better!

So, rattle those pots and pans, my medium-size angels, and get to creating memories and delicious dishes in your kitchen! With love, from my kitchen to yours,

Paula Deen
Savannah, Georgia
September 2009

A Note to Chefs

Now you are ready to start cooking for your family, for yourself, and for your friends.

In creating this cookbook, I tried to think of the events that you might have during a school year—a sleepover, a bake sale to raise money for some worthy cause (like new cheerleader uniforms or money to assist a needy family at Christmas), and a party for the cast of your play or the football team. I also included some recipes that you can take to school—muffins for busy mornings and some delicious new ideas for your lunch box.

At your age, you are still doing lots of things with your parents, thank goodness. So I've got some recipes for Mother's Day and Father's Day, and a menu for a family picnic to the beach or park. I also thought about a Christmas cooking party, where you can make gifts with your friends for your other friends. I think you are going to love my favorite chapter—a family cooking night, when the family plans, shops for, and prepares dinner together. Talk about making memories!

In my first children's cookbook, I included one special section on manners. In this cookbook, I've included manners with each chapter. I believe strongly in good manners. In the South, manners have always been important, and they still are today.

Another thing that's a little different about this book: There is also a cooking lesson that goes with the recipes in each chapter. The lessons offer specific advice about making each group of recipes.

So, if you start at the front of the book and work your way through, you will develop as a cook and practice good manners along the way. Isn't that great?

Table of

Contents

Cooking Tips

Keeping my little cooks safe is very important to me. So, please, promise me you'll use this little cheat sheet for safety in the kitchen.

⭐ Always have an adult available to assist you. As your cooking skills develop, you will be able to do more and more by yourself, but you should cook only when an adult is in the kitchen with you.

⭐ When cutting, use a cutting board to cut on, never the countertop.

⭐ When using sharp knives (meaning knives other than the butter knives you use every day at the table), let an adult help you.

⭐ Ask for help when cutting hard foods, especially round ones like potatoes. You may not have the hand strength to chop these, and they can be tricky and roll around on the cutting board!

⭐ Always cut away from yourself, never toward your body.

⭐ Wash your hands
- before getting started,
- every time you touch your mouth or nose,
- and after you've worked with raw chicken or beef.

⭐ Wear an apron or smock to protect your clothes.

⭐ If you have long hair, tie it back so it won't get caught in the soup pot or on a burner! Also, this will keep your hair from getting in people's food!

⭐ Don't wear long, flowing sleeves—they can get caught on pot handles or drag in your sauté pan.

⭐ Use oven mitts to remove pans from the oven and to take lids off of pots.

⭐ If you are short, use a step stool so that you are at a comfortable height for cutting and cooking.

⭐ Always cook in closed-toe shoes to protect your feet from hot liquids, broken glass, or dropped cans!

⭐ Keep a pan of hot, soapy water ready so that you can wash your dishes as you go. Cooking also means cleaning up!

⭐ Take this tip from the cooking pros: Assemble everything you will need for the recipe before you start. Read through the recipe once before you begin it. This will make the recipe go much smoother.

Glossary

Here are all the vocabulary words you'll need to know if you are going to become a good cook. Lots of these are the same as those in *My First Cookbook*, but I thought you might need a refresher. The best part? You don't have to take a vocabulary test on these!

 BAKE—Cook in the oven. There are top and bottom burners, and the heat from baking comes from the ones in the bottom of the oven.

 BEAT—Mix with a spoon or a mixer until two or more ingredients are smooth.

 BOIL—Cook on the cooktop in a pot until you see bubbles. The hotter the temperature, the bigger the bubbles.

 BROIL—Cook in a very hot oven until the top gets browned and bubbly. The heat from broiling comes from the burners in the top of the oven. You usually leave the oven door open a crack when you broil.

 CHOP—Cut food into pieces with a knife. The recipe will tell you if the pieces should be big or small.

 CUBE—Cut food into little squares all the same size.

DICE—Cut food into teeny pieces all the same size.

 FLOUR—There are several types of flour—all-purpose, self-rising, and bread flour, just to name a few. Be sure to use the kind recommended in the recipe. Sometimes, a recipe will tell you to "flour" a pan, which means that you will put about a tablespoon of flour into a buttered pan and shake the pan until the flour coats all the sides and the bottom of the pan.

 FOLD—Stir gently (the opposite of "beat") with a rubber spatula, going deep into the batter and lifting it over on top of itself, mixing well.

 FONDUE—This is food cooked in a special pot in the center of the table. I have recipes for both chocolate and cheese fondue. I do not recommend that you attempt to fry in a fondue pot until you are older.

 GARNISH—Edible decoration—a little sprig of parsley, or a slice of lemon or a berry—that you put on a plate before you serve whatever it is you cooked.

 GRATE—Rub food against a grater to make slivers of food. Watch your fingers and fingernails!

 GREASE—Grease is fat, like bacon grease. When the directions tell you to "grease" the pan, you rub the fat, such as butter or shortening, over the inside surface of the pan.

KNEAD—This is a fun activity where you take dough and slap it on your countertop, press into it with both palms, then pull the top over and turn the dough. Do it again and again and again! Sometimes (usually), you have to add a little flour to the dough to keep it from sticking.

MELT—Heat something solid, like butter, until it becomes a liquid.

MINCE—This is like "dice," only smaller—cut food into tiny pieces that are all the same size.

PAN-FRY—This is cooking food on the cooktop in a skillet in a little oil or butter. You typically only turn the food once or twice to get a crisp exterior.

PEEL—Pull off the skin of a fruit, such as a banana or an orange, or the shell from a hard-cooked egg, or cut off the skin of a vegetable or fruit, such as a potato or an apple.

ROLL OUT—Flatten with a rolling pin or your fingertips— usually biscuits, bread, or pizza dough.

SAUTÉ—This is almost the same as "pan-fry." Cook in a skillet on the cooktop in a small amount of fat. The difference is that when you pan-fry, you usually don't turn the food but once or twice. When you sauté, you keep turning it over and over until all the food gets done.

SCRAPE DOWN—When mixing food, take a rubber spatula and scrape down all of the food on the sides of the bowl so that it gets mixed in good.

 SIFT—Put dry ingredients in a sifter and turn the handle until all of the stuff (like flour) gets mixed up and comes out of the holes in the bottom.

 SIMMER—Cook in a pot on the cooktop over low heat until there are tiny bubbles all around the sides of the pot.

 SPRINKLE—Take one ingredient and scatter it lightly over the top of something else.

 STIR—Mix with a spoon.

 TOSS—Mix ingredients very gently.

 WHIP—Use a mixer to beat something vigorously, like cream or egg whites. This is super fun!

 WHISK—A whisk is an instrument that looks like the beaters on an electric mixer. You use it to mix things like eggs and to stir sauces so they will be smooth. When a recipe says to "whisk" something, you use a whisk to stir.

How to Measure

Measuring is important when you cook. You can't just guess—you have to use the exact amount that the recipe tells you to if you want your cookies and cupcakes to taste good.

DRY

LIQUID

There are two types of measuring cups: One type is used for dry ingredients, and the other is used for liquid ingredients. However, sometimes the "dry" ingredients aren't dry: You use a "dry" measuring cup to measure mayonnaise and sour cream.

Cup sizes
One-fourth (¼)
One-third (⅓)
One-half (½)
One cup

To measure white sugar and flour
Dip the dry-type measuring cup into the flour and fill it until it is heaping full. Take the back of a butter knife and scrape off the top until it is level.

To measure brown sugar
Spoon the brown sugar into the measuring cup you use for dry ingredients and pat down until the sugar is even with the top of the cup. You do this just like you do wet sand in a bucket on the beach. When you turn the sugar out, it should be in the shape of the cup.

To measure butter
Butter has measuring marks on the wrapper so you can just cut off what you need.
One-fourth (¼) stick equals two tablespoons
One-half (½) stick equals one-fourth (¼) cup

Six tablespoons equals one-third (⅓) cup
One stick equals one-half (½) cup
Two sticks equal one cup

To measure cut-up foods

Cut them up first, then place them into the measuring cup you use for dry ingredients until they reach the top of the cup.

To measure liquids

Use a liquid measuring cup and put it on the counter. Stand so that your eyes are even with the cup. Pour in the water, juice, milk, or oil until it reaches the line exactly on the cup.

To measure salt

Stand by the sink and pour the salt into the measuring spoon. Level it with your fingertips.

To measure baking powder, baking soda, pepper, and cinnamon or other spices

Dip the measuring spoon into the container and get a heaping spoonful of whatever you are measuring. Press the spoon against the side of the container and pull out the spoon—the ingredient will be packed into the spoon. Or you can level off the ingredients with the back of a butter knife, or the side of your finger!

To measure liquids in a spoon

Pour them into the spoon over the sink or a bowl or cup until they reach the top. Have the bowl you are adding them to nearby so you won't have to walk with the liquid in the spoon.

Morning

Muffins

Why in the world does school start so early? And who has time to eat when you've got to look hip and locate that dad-gum overstuffed book bag? And who invented homework, anyway? Getting out the door to get to school on time involves lots of hustle and bustle. By the time you get to school, you are just beginning to wake up, and you realize you're starving!

Do I have a solution for you! Try one of my morning muffins! These muffins are designed to take the place of the breakfast you didn't have time to eat. You can eat them during the car ride to school, on the bus if your bus driver allows snacking, or in the lunchroom while you're waiting for the morning bell. Each muffin is chock-full of good-for-you ingredients.

Here's an idea: Make a batch of each muffin recipe one Saturday (it will take you most of the day, but if you do it with a buddy, it's really fun). Label gallon freezer bags with the name of each type of muffin, and freeze them. Then you can just pull the muffins from the freezer when you're heading out the door. They thaw in 45 seconds in the microwave, or in about 30 minutes in a plastic bag.

Muffin Manners

- Take two and share with a friend.
- Grab a napkin to catch the crumbs. Always pick up your crumbs and throw away the plastic bag your muffin came in. Don't be a litterbug!
- You might want to pack a breath mint if you eat a frittata muffin or a sausage cheese muffin.

Cooking Lesson

When making muffins, mix together all of the dry ingredients, then make a "well" in the center of the dry ingredients with a spoon. Combine all of the liquid ingredients in another bowl, and pour them into the center of the well. Then mix the wet and the dry ingredients together just until the dry ingredients are moistened. The mixture will be lumpy. Overmixing makes tough muffins. We found that our muffins did better baked in muffin pans sprayed with nonstick cooking spray than they did when baked in paper liners.

P.S. Muffins are also great for sleepovers (serve them with fresh fruit) and for snacking on road trips. Better than cookies because they're healthier. Well, not better. Just healthier.

Apple Raisin Muffins

These are good for you!

 Muffin pan

 Dry measuring cups

 Medium bowl

 Liquid measuring cup

 Measuring spoons

 Whisk

 Fork

 Large bowl

 Rubber spatula

 Oven mitts

 Wire rack

 Cooking spray

 2 cups apples, peeled, cored, and finely diced
(about 3 medium apples)

 1 cup sugar

 ⅓ cup canola oil

 2 eggs, beaten

 1 teaspoon vanilla extract

 1½ cups unbleached all-purpose flour

 1 teaspoon baking soda

 1 teaspoon baking powder

 ½ teaspoon salt

 1 teaspoon cinnamon

 ⅓ cup raisins
(one 1½-ounce box)

 ¼ cup chopped pecans

1. Position oven rack in middle of oven. Preheat the oven to 375 degrees. Spray 12 muffin cups with cooking spray.

2. Place the apples and sugar in a medium bowl and toss together. In a large measuring cup, measure the oil, then add the eggs and vanilla extract. Mix well with a whisk. Pour the oil-egg mixture into the apple mixture and stir well with a fork.

3. In a large bowl, combine the flour, baking soda, baking powder, salt, and cinnamon. Stir well with a fork. Add the raisins and pecans, and stir well with a fork. Make a well in the center of the dry ingredients. Pour the apple mixture over the flour mixture and stir with a fork until all of the dry ingredients are mixed in. You can use a spatula to scrape the sides of the bowl. Don't overmix. Batter is *very* thick!

4. Use a ⅓-cup dry measuring cup to fill the muffin pan, dividing the batter evenly among the cups.

5. Bake the muffins for 18 to 20 minutes, until lightly browned and the sides pull away from the muffin cups.

6. Have an adult help you remove the muffin pan from the oven and place it on a wire rack to cool. After 5 minutes, remove the muffins from the pan and place them on the wire rack to cool completely, about 30 minutes.

7. Place the muffins in a labeled freezer bag and store in the freezer.

8. When you want a muffin, remove directly from the freezer and place in a plastic sandwich bag. The muffin will be thawed in about 30 minutes. Or you can place it in the microwave oven for 45 seconds to thaw.

Makes 12 muffins

Banana Nut Muffins

Like banana bread? You'll love these muffins!

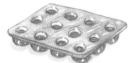

Muffin pan — Medium bowl — Liquid measuring cup — Dry measuring cups — Whisk

Large bowl — Measuring spoons — Fork — Rubber spatula — Oven mitts

Wire rack — Cooking spray

1 cup mashed banana
(about 2 medium bananas)

2 eggs, beaten

³/₄ cup sugar — ½ cup canola oil — ½ teaspoon cinnamon — ½ teaspoon baking powder — 1 teaspoon baking soda

³/₄ cup whole wheat flour — ³/₄ cup unbleached all-purpose flour — ¼ cup chopped pecans — ⅓ cup raisins (one 1½-ounce box)

1. Position oven rack in middle of oven. Preheat the oven to 375 degrees. Spray 12 muffin cups with cooking spray.

2. In a medium bowl, mix together the mashed bananas, eggs, sugar, and oil with a whisk.

3. In a large bowl, combine the cinnamon, baking powder, baking soda, whole wheat flour, and all-purpose flour. Stir with a fork until mixed. Stir in the pecans and raisins. Make a well in the center of the dry ingredients. Pour the banana mixture into the flour mixture and stir with a fork until all of the dry ingredients are mixed in. You can use a spatula to scrape down the sides of the bowl. Don't overmix.

4. Use a ⅓-cup dry measuring cup to fill the muffin pan, dividing the batter evenly among the cups.

5. Bake the muffins for 18 to 20 minutes, until lightly browned and the sides pull away from the muffin cups.

6. Have an adult help you remove the muffin pan from the oven and place it on a wire rack to cool. After 5 minutes, remove the muffins from the pan and place them on the wire rack to cool completely, about 30 minutes.

7. Place the muffins in a labeled freezer bag and store in the freezer.

8. When you want a muffin, remove directly from the freezer and place in a plastic sandwich bag. The muffin will be thawed in about 30 minutes. Or you can place it in the microwave oven for 45 seconds to thaw.

Makes 12 muffins

Raisin Bran Muffins

Make these as gifts for Grandma and Grandpa.

 Muffin pan

 Large bowl

 Dry measuring cups

 Measuring spoons

 Fork

 Medium bowl

 Liquid measuring cup

 Whisk

 Rubber spatula

 Oven mitts

 Wire rack

 Cooking spray

 2 cups raisin bran cereal

 2 cups unbleached all-purpose flour

 ½ cup sugar

 ⅓ cup chopped pecans

 1 teaspoon baking soda

 ½ teaspoon salt

 1 egg, beaten

 1 cup buttermilk

 ¼ cup canola oil

1. Position oven rack in the middle of the oven. Preheat the oven to 375 degrees. Spray 12 muffin cups with cooking spray.

2. In a large mixing bowl, combine the cereal, flour, sugar, pecans, baking soda, and salt. Stir together with a fork. Make a well in the center of the dry ingredients.

3. In a medium bowl, combine the egg, buttermilk, and oil. Whisk until well combined. Pour the egg mixture into the dry mixture and stir with a fork until all of the dry ingredients are mixed in. Use a spatula to scrape down the sides. Don't overmix.

4. Use a $\frac{1}{3}$-cup dry measuring cup to fill the muffin pan, dividing the batter evenly among the cups.

5. Bake the muffins for 18 to 20 minutes, until lightly browned and the sides pull away from the muffin cups.

6. Have an adult help you remove the muffin pan from the oven and place it on a wire rack to cool. After 5 minutes, remove the muffins from the pan and place them on the wire rack to cool completely, about 30 minutes.

7. Place the muffins in a labeled freezer bag and store in the freezer.

8. When you want a muffin, remove directly from the freezer and place in a plastic sandwich bag. The muffin will be thawed in about 30 minutes. Or you can place it in the microwave oven for 45 seconds to thaw.

Makes 12 muffins

Peanut Butter–Oatmeal Muffins

Protein and oatmeal will get your day off to a good start.

Muffin pan   Large bowl   Dry measuring cups   Measuring spoons   Fork

Medium bowl   Liquid measuring cup   Whisk   Rubber spatula   Oven mitts

Wire rack   Cooking spray   1½ cups unbleached all-purpose flour   ½ cup quick-cooking rolled oats

1 teaspoon baking powder   ¼ teaspoon baking soda   ¼ teaspoon salt   1 cup packed brown sugar

½ cup chunky peanut butter   2 eggs, beaten   1 cup buttermilk

1. Position oven rack in the middle of the oven. Preheat the oven to 375 degrees. Spray 12 muffin cups with cooking spray.

2. In a large mixing bowl, stir together the flour, oats, baking powder, baking soda, salt, and brown sugar. Stir well with a fork. Make a well in the center of the dry ingredients.

3. In a medium mixing bowl, combine the peanut butter, eggs, and buttermilk, and whisk gently until very smooth. Pour the peanut butter mixture into the dry mixture and stir with a fork until all of the dry ingredients are mixed in. Use a spatula to scrape down the sides of the bowl. Don't overmix.

4. Use a $\frac{1}{3}$-cup dry measuring cup to fill the muffin pan, dividing the batter evenly among the cups.

5. Bake the muffins for 18 to 20 minutes, until lightly browned and the sides pull away from the muffin cups.

6. Have an adult help you remove the muffin pan from the oven and place it on a wire rack to cool. After 5 minutes, remove the muffins from the pan and place them on the wire rack to cool completely, about 30 minutes.

7. Place the muffins in a labeled freezer bag and store in the freezer.

8. When you want a muffin, remove directly from the freezer and place in a plastic sandwich bag. The muffin will be thawed in about 30 minutes. Or you can place it in the microwave oven for 45 seconds to thaw.

Makes 12 muffins

Blueberry Buttermilk Muffins

Pick the blueberries yourself and these are even better!

Muffin pan | Large bowl | Dry measuring cups | Measuring spoons | Fork

Liquid measuring cup | Whisk | Rubber spatula | Oven mitts | Wire rack

Cooking spray | 1³/₄ cups fresh (or frozen) blueberries | 2 cups unbleached all-purpose flour | 2 teaspoons baking powder | 1 teaspoon salt

1 cup sugar | ¹/₃ cup canola oil | 1 cup buttermilk | 2 eggs, beaten | 1 teaspoon vanilla extract

1. Position oven rack in the middle of the oven. Preheat the oven to 400 degrees. Spray 12 muffin cups with cooking spray.

2. Pick through the blueberries and remove any that are moldy or smushed. In a large bowl, place the flour, baking powder, salt, and sugar and stir with a fork until combined. Put the blueberries in the dry mixture and toss to coat the blueberries. Make a well in the dry ingredients.

3. In a large liquid measuring cup, measure the oil, then the buttermilk. Add the eggs and the vanilla extract and whisk until blended. Pour the wet ingredients into the well in the dry ingredients. Stir with a fork until all of the dry ingredients are mixed in. Use a spatula to scrape down the sides of the bowl. Don't overmix.

4. Use a ⅓-cup dry measuring cup to fill the muffin pan, dividing the batter evenly among the cups.

5. Bake the muffins for 18 to 20 minutes, until lightly browned and the sides pull away from the muffin cups.

6. Have an adult help you remove the muffin pan from the oven and place it on a wire rack to cool. After 5 minutes, remove the muffins from the pan and place them on the wire rack to cool completely, about 30 minutes.

7. Place the muffins in a labeled freezer bag and store in the freezer.

8. When you want a muffin, remove directly from the freezer and place in a plastic sandwich bag. The muffin will be thawed in about 30 minutes. Or you can place it in the microwave oven for 45 seconds to thaw.

Makes 12 muffins

Frittata Muffins

A frittata is just an omelette with the ingredients folded in.

Muffin pan

Small skillet

Dry measuring cups

Wooden spoon

Liquid measuring cup

Measuring spoons

Whisk

Oven mitts

Wire rack

Cooking spray

¼ cup finely chopped onion

½ cup finely chopped ham

²/₃ cup shredded sharp Cheddar cheese

4 eggs, beaten

½ teaspoon salt

¼ teaspoon pepper

1. Position oven rack in the middle of the oven. Preheat the oven to 350 degrees. Spray 6 muffin cups with cooking spray.

2. Spray a small skillet with cooking spray. Have an adult help you sauté the onions in the skillet over low heat until the onions are soft, about 5 minutes. Add the ham and sauté until the ham begins to brown, about 3 minutes.

3. Distribute the onions and ham evenly into the prepared muffin cups. Using your fingers, distribute the cheese evenly into the muffin cups. In a large liquid measuring cup, combine the eggs, salt, and pepper and whisk until very smooth. Pour the egg mixture over the cheese in the muffin cups, dividing the egg mixture evenly among the cups. (Use a teaspoon to take a little out of one cup and add it to another cup if you mess up.)

4. Bake the muffins for 20 minutes, or until set. Have an adult help you remove the muffin pan from the oven and place it on a wire rack to cool. After 5 minutes, remove muffins from the pan and place them on the wire rack to cool completely. It will take about 30 minutes. Muffins will puff up during cooking, then deflate while they are cooling.

5. Keep muffins refrigerated (they will keep for 3 to 4 days in the refrigerator). When you are ready to eat one, reheat it in the microwave for about 8 seconds. You will probably want to pack two for your breakfast. Pack along a breath mint! Delicious, but the onions and eggs do stay with you!

Makes 6 muffins

Sausage Cheese Muffins

These are best eaten within a few days.

Muffin pan

Medium skillet

Wooden spoon

Large bowl

Dry measuring cups

Measuring spoons

Fork

Liquid measuring cup

Whisk

Rubber spatula

Oven mitts

Wire rack

Cooking spray

1 cup crumbled mild sausage, sautéed until no pink remains, and drained

2 cups unbleached all-purpose flour

1 tablespoon baking powder

½ teaspoon salt

¼ teaspoon pepper

1 cup milk

⅓ cup canola oil

2 eggs, beaten

1½ cups shredded sharp Cheddar cheese

32

1. Position oven rack in the middle of the oven. Preheat the oven to 375 degrees. Spray 12 muffin cups with cooking spray.

2. Have an adult help you sauté sausage in a medium skillet, breaking it up with a wooden spoon over medium heat until no pink remains, about 7 minutes. Have an adult drain the fat from the pan.

3. In a large bowl, combine the flour, baking powder, salt, and pepper. Stir with a fork until blended. Make a well in the center of the dry ingredients.

4. In a large liquid measuring cup, measure the milk and oil. Add the eggs and beat well with a whisk. Pour the liquid ingredients into the dry ingredients and stir with a fork until all of the dry ingredients are mixed in. Use a spatula to scrape down the sides of the bowl. Don't overmix. Fold in the sausage. Then add the cheese and stir again.

5. Use a ⅓-cup dry measuring cup to fill the muffin pan, dividing the batter evenly among the cups.

6. Bake the muffins for 20 to 22 minutes, until lightly browned and the sides pull away from the muffin cups.

7. Have an adult help you remove the muffin pan from the oven and place it on a wire rack to cool. After 5 minutes, remove the muffins from the pan and place them on the wire rack to cool completely, about 30 minutes.

8. Place the muffins in a labeled freezer bag and store in the freezer.

9. When you want a muffin, remove directly from the freezer and place in a plastic sandwich bag. The muffin will be thawed in about 30 minutes. You can then heat it up in the microwave oven for about 15 seconds. Or you can place it in the microwave oven for 45 seconds to thaw.

Makes 12 muffins

CHAPTER TWO
The Bake

Sale

Everybody loves a bake sale! It is a great way to raise quick cash for a good cause. Whether you are buying new cheerleader uniforms or mosquito nets to send to Africa, you can expect to make a couple of hundred dollars with some careful planning and the right items on your bake sale menu. Here's what I suggest:

- A good variety of delicious cookies; don't forget everyone's favorite: chocolate chip!
- Chocolate-covered pretzels—got to love that sweet-salty blend.
- Brownies—if you're selling to kids, I'd skip the nuts.
- A yummy-looking cake that you sell by the slice.
- A hearty pie, which you also can sell by the slice.
- Cupcakes, decorated with sprinkles or garnishes to match the season!
- I love pumpkin, so I'm throwing in a pumpkin roll that you can sell by the slice.

Here are some tips for a successful bake sale.

Plan your menu carefully with your sponsor (usually a teacher, club leader, Scout leader, or coach). Line up your volunteers well in advance. Make sure everyone knows what they're baking, and where and when they'll be expected to be on the day of the sale. Ask permission to have the sale at school, at a sports event, or in front of a department store.

Purchase the following items at the dollar store:

- A plastic table cover—you can throw it away at the end of the day.
- Small paper plates and plastic forks for the cakes and pies.
- Napkins for the customers and paper towels for your group.

There are a few things you'll need to do ahead of time:

- Print out a big sign with prices. Price items in round numbers so you don't have to make change—$1 per cupcake, for example. Set the sign on a photo stand, or tape it to the edge of the table.
- Decorate your table to reflect the theme of your sale—use helium balloons on either side of the table, and have the artistic members of the group create a large sign to hang behind the bake sale table. Consider having the members of your group wear uniforms or dress alike in some way—wearing Santa hats during a holiday bake sale, for example.
- Remind the sponsor to bring a knife to cut the cakes and pies. Always let the adults handle sharp knives. Get the sponsor to cut all of the cakes and pies at once, and then give the knife to the principal for safekeeping.

Here are things you should have on hand:

- Keep a wet cloth in a plastic bag to use for spills, etc.
- Have a bottle of hand sanitizer handy to use throughout the day.
- Bring extra sandwich-size plastic bags in the event one of your volunteers forgets to wrap the merchandise individually. Packaging is very important. Two beautiful chocolate chip cookies in a plastic bag will sell better than two crumbly cookies sitting on a plate.
- If someone is bringing cupcakes, have a tray or container with a lid on hand to keep insects away.
- Have a trash can or trash bags handy for customers.
- Have fun! Remind your customers that they are giving to a good cause!

Bake Sale Manners

- If you promise the bake sale organizer that you will bake something, keep your promise! You can't have a bake sale if everyone forgets to bring their stuff in.
- Wash your hands before you start the sale. Let one person handle the money—he or she shouldn't touch the food afterward. Use a napkin or plastic gloves to pick up the food for your customers.
- Don't taste any of the merchandise! It's for the customers! If something's left at the end, you can buy it. Remember, it's all about making money for a worthy cause.
- Be polite to your customers. "May I help you?" and "Thank you for supporting us" are the phrases of the day! Oh, and if you run out of something, try this line: "I am so sorry! We'll make more of those next time!"

Cooking Lesson

When baking cookies, use parchment paper to line your cookie sheets. The cookies will brown more evenly, and the bottoms won't burn (unless you leave the cookies in the oven too long, silly!) Once the cookies come out of the oven, let them cool for several minutes on the cookie sheet so that they firm up before you try to transfer them with a spatula to a wire rack to cool completely. Store them in an airtight container until you're ready to package them for selling.

Peanut Butter Cookies

These are very crisp and not too sweet.

 Large bowl

 Dry measuring cups

 Measuring spoons

 Electric mixer

 Small bowl

 Sifter

 Cookie sheet

 Parchment paper

 Fork

 Oven mitts

 Wide spatula

 Wire racks

 1 cup shortening

 ½ teaspoon salt

 1 cup smooth peanut butter

 1 cup sugar

 1 cup packed brown sugar

 2 eggs, beaten

 1 tablespoon whole milk

 2 cups unbleached all-purpose flour

½ teaspoon baking soda

1. Preheat the oven to 325 degrees.

2. Cream the shortening, salt, and peanut butter in a large bowl with an electric mixer until very smooth. Add the sugar and brown sugar, and continue to beat until creamy. Add the eggs and whole milk, and beat again. In a small bowl, sift together the flour and baking soda. Add it to the peanut butter mixture, and beat until smooth.

3. Roll the batter into walnut-size balls. Place them 1½ inches apart on a cookie sheet lined with parchment paper. Press the balls lightly with a fork. Then press across the other way with the fork. This makes a pretty crisscross pattern. If the fork gets stuck, dip it into a little sugar before pressing into the cookie.

4. Bake for 15 to 20 minutes, until lightly browned. Have an adult help you remove the cookies from the oven; allow them to sit for 2 minutes, then remove them to wire racks to cool completely. Store in airtight containers until ready to package for the sale.

Makes about 4 dozen cookies

Chocolate Chip Cookies

You cannot have enough of these at a bake sale. They are perfect.

Large bowl

Dry measuring cups

Measuring spoons

Electric mixer

Small bowl

Sifter

Wooden spoon

Parchment paper

Cookie sheet

Oven mitts

Wide spatula

Wire racks

2 sticks butter, at room temperature

3/4 cup packed brown sugar

3/4 cup sugar

1 teaspoon vanilla extract

2 eggs, beaten

2 cups unbleached all-purpose flour

1 teaspoon baking soda

1 teaspoon salt

One 12-ounce package semisweet chocolate chips

1. Preheat the oven to 375 degrees.

2. In a large bowl, combine the butter, brown sugar, sugar, vanilla extract, and ½ teaspoon water, and beat with an electric mixer until light and fluffy. Add the eggs and beat again. In a small bowl, sift together the flour, baking soda, and salt. Blend the dry ingredients into the butter mixture with a wooden spoon, then beat with the electric mixer until combined. Stir in the chocolate chips with the spoon.

3. Drop the dough by tablespoons at least 2 inches apart on a parchment-lined cookie sheet. Bake for 8 to 10 minutes, until golden.

4. Have an adult help you remove the cookies from the oven; allow them to sit for 1 minute, then remove them to wire racks to cool completely. Store in airtight containers until ready to package for the sale.

Makes about 4 dozen cookies

Chocolate-Covered Pretzels

Pretzels, chocolate, and sprinkles? A perfect combination.

Measuring
spoons

2 small glass
bowls

Wooden
spoon

Butter knife

Oven mitts

Waxed paper

One 6-ounce package
chocolate chips
(milk chocolate or semisweet,
whichever you like!)

2 tablespoons
shortening

48 large
pretzel rods

One 10½-ounce
container rainbow
sprinkles

One 6-ounce
package white
chocolate chips

1. Melt the chocolate chips and 1 tablespoon shortening in a small glass bowl for 1 minute on high power in a microwave oven. Have an adult help you remove the bowl from the microwave oven. Stir. If the morsels aren't quite melted enough, microwave them for 15 seconds more. Dip three-quarters of one pretzel into the chocolate. Use a butter knife to help scrape off any excess from the bottom of the pretzel. Lay the pretzel on waxed paper to dry. Sprinkle with sprinkles while chocolate is still warm. Repeat with 23 more pretzels.

2. Then melt the white chocolate morsels and 1 tablespoon shortening in another small glass bowl for 1 minute on high power in a microwave oven. Have an adult help you remove the bowl from the microwave oven. Stir. If the morsels aren't quite melted enough, microwave them for 15 seconds more. Dip three-quarters of one pretzel into the chocolate. Use a butter knife to help scrape off any excess from the bottom of the pretzel. Lay the pretzel on waxed paper to dry. Sprinkle with sprinkles while chocolate is still warm. Repeat with 23 more pretzels.

3. Pretzels take about an hour to dry completely. Store in airtight containers until ready to package for the sale.

Makes 48 pretzels

Brownies

These are chewy, with a rich chocolate flavor.

8-inch square
cake pan

Electric
mixer

Dry measuring cups

Small glass
bowl

Wooden
spoon

Small bowl

Measuring
spoons

Sifter

Oven mitts

Wire rack

Cooking
spray

2 eggs

1 cup sugar

3 squares
unsweetened
chocolate

⅓ cup
vegetable
shortening

½ cup
unbleached
all-purpose flour

½ teaspoon
baking powder

⅛ teaspoon
salt

1 teaspoon
vanilla extract

1. Preheat the oven to 325 degrees. Spray an 8-inch square cake pan with cooking spray.

2. Beat the eggs with an electric mixer until thick. Add the sugar and beat until smooth.

3. Put the chocolate and shortening in a small glass bowl, and microwave on high power for 1 minute. Have an adult help you remove the bowl from the microwave oven. Stir. If the chocolate is not melted, microwave it for 15 seconds more, then stir again. Add the chocolate to the eggs.

4. In a small bowl, sift together the flour, baking powder, and salt. Add the dry ingredients to the chocolate mixture. Add the vanilla extract. Mix well with the electric mixer.

5. Spread the batter evenly into the cake pan. Bake for 28 minutes. Have an adult help you remove the pan from the oven and place it on a wire rack to cool completely. Your adult helper can then cut the brownies into 16 pieces. Store them in airtight containers until ready to package for the sale.

Makes 16 brownies

Strawberry Cake with Strawberry Icing

This is perfect for a holiday or Valentine's Day sale.
The weather needs to be chilly or the icing will run.

 Three 9-inch round cake pans

 Measuring spoons

 Dry measuring cups

 Liquid measuring cup

 Large bowl

 Electric mixer

 Rubber spatula

 Oven mitts

 Wire racks

 Butter knife

 Dinner plate

 Medium bowl

 Cake plate

 Cooking spray

 Flour for dusting pans

 One 18¼-ounce package yellow cake mix

 One 3-ounce package strawberry gelatin

 1 cup mashed strawberries, with their juice

 1 cup vegetable oil

 ½ cup low-fat milk

4 eggs

 8 ounces cream cheese, at room temperature

 1 stick butter, at room temperature

 3½ cups confectioners' sugar, sifted

 ½ cup mashed strawberries, drained

1. Preheat the oven to 350 degrees. Spray three 9-inch round cake pans with cooking spray, then put about 1 tablespoon of flour in each pan and tap the pan on all sides to distribute the flour. Dump out any excess flour into the trash can.

2. Place the cake mix, gelatin, strawberries with their juice, oil, milk, and eggs in a large bowl, and blend with an electric mixer on low speed until combined. Scrape down the bowl with a rubber spatula, and mix until the batter is very smooth. Divide the batter evenly into the three pans, and then smooth out the batter.

3. Bake the cakes in the center of the oven for 20 to 22 minutes, until the cakes look set in the center and begin to pull away from the pans. Have an adult help you remove the pans from the oven, and allow them to sit on a wire rack for about 15 minutes undisturbed. Next, run a butter knife around the edge of each cake and invert the cakes one by one onto a dinner plate, then turn them back over onto a wire rack, right side up, to cool completely.

4. Meanwhile, make the icing by placing the cream cheese and butter into a medium bowl and mixing with an electric mixer until smooth. Add the confectioners' sugar and the drained strawberries (if you don't drain them, your icing will be too runny). Beat on low until combined.

5. Place one cake layer on a cake plate and ice the top with a clean butter knife. Repeat with the second and third layers. Then ice the sides. Place the cake plate in the refrigerator until the icing has firmed up, about an hour.

6. For the bake sale, you can take the whole cake to the sale if you have some way to transport it safely. Or you can slice the whole cake into about 16 slices and place each slice side by side in a covered container. Keep refrigerated until ready for the sale. Do not place the slices in a plastic bag or the icing will get yucky.

Makes 1 cake, which yields about 16 slices

Pumpkin Roll with Cream Cheese Icing

This is especially good for Halloween or Thanksgiving sales.

10-by-15-inch rimmed baking sheet

Parchment paper

Large bowl

Dry measuring cups

Electric mixer

Small bowl

Sifter

Measuring spoons

Rubber spatula

Oven mitts

Kitchen towel

Medium bowl

Butter knife

Waxed paper

Cooking spray

... 3 eggs

1 cup sugar

2/3 cup pureed pumpkin

3/4 cup unbleached all-purpose flour

1 teaspoon baking powder

2 teaspoons cinnamon

1 teaspoon nutmeg

1/2 teaspoon salt

8 ounces cream cheese, at room temperature

1 stick butter, at room temperature

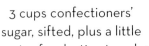
3 cups confectioners' sugar, sifted, plus a little extra for dusting towel

1 teaspoon vanilla extract

1. Preheat the oven to 375 degrees. Line the rimmed baking sheet with parchment paper. Spray the paper and the sides of the pan with cooking spray.

2. In a large bowl, combine the eggs and sugar. Beat with an electric mixer for 5 minutes. Add the pumpkin and mix well. In a small bowl, sift together the flour, baking powder, cinnamon, nutmeg, and salt. Add the dry mixture to the wet mixture and mix well, scraping down the sides of the bowl with a rubber spatula several times. Mix until smooth, about 2 minutes.

3. Spread the batter on the baking sheet, and smooth with the spatula. Bake for 12 to 15 minutes, until the top appears set and the cake pulls away from the sides of the pan. Have an adult help you remove the baking sheet from the oven, and allow the cake to sit undisturbed for about 3 minutes. Turn the cake out onto a kitchen towel that has been sprinkled with confectioners' sugar. Starting at the narrow end, roll up the cake in the towel and let it cool completely, seam side down, for 1 hour.

4. Meanwhile, in a medium bowl, combine the cream cheese and butter, and beat with an electric mixer until smooth. Add the confectioners' sugar and vanilla extract, and beat until smooth.

5. Carefully unroll the cake, and spread the icing over it with a clean butter knife. Reroll the cake (without the towel!), and place the cake, seam side down, on waxed paper. Wrap tightly and keep in the refrigerator. You can take the whole cake to the bake sale and slice it there, or slice it at home and place the slices side by side in a covered container.

Makes 1 roll, which yields about 10 slices

Chocolate Chip Cake

This is beautiful with just a dusting of confectioners' sugar.

 Bundt pan

 Measuring spoons

 Large bowl

 Dry measuring cups

 Liquid measuring cup

 Electric mixer

 Wooden spoon

 Oven mitts

 Butter knife

 Wire rack

 Strainer

 Cooking spray

 Flour for dusting pan

 One 18¼-ounce package yellow cake mix

 1 cup sour cream

 4 eggs

 ½ cup vegetable oil

 One 3-ounce package instant chocolate pudding mix

 One 12-ounce package semisweet chocolate chips

 Confectioners' sugar to dust the top of the cake

1. Preheat the oven to 350 degrees. Spray a Bundt pan with cooking spray, then put about 2 tablespoons of flour in the bottom of the pan. Tap the pan and turn it all around until the flour coats all surfaces of the pan. Dump out any excess flour into the trash can.

2. In a large bowl, combine the cake mix, sour cream, eggs, oil, and pudding mix. Combine with an electric mixer until very smooth. Stir in the chocolate chips.

3. Place the batter evenly in the Bundt pan and smooth the top. Bake for 45 to 50 minutes, until the top appears set and the cake begins to pull away from the sides of the pan. Have an adult help you remove the pan from the oven. Allow the cake to cool in the pan for about 15 minutes, then take a butter knife and run it around the side of the pan. Invert the cake onto a wire rack to cool completely.

4. Dust the top of the cake by placing confectioners' sugar into a strainer, holding it above the cake, and tapping the sides of the strainer. Move the strainer from place to place until the cake is dusted.

5. When the cake is cool, you can wrap it in plastic wrap, take it to the sale, and cut it there into 16 pieces. Or you can cut it at home and place the slices side by side in an airtight container or store in plastic bags.

Makes 1 cake, which yields about 16 slices

German Chocolate Pies

Adults will love a slice of this pie.

Large bowl

Dry measuring cups

Measuring spoons

Electric mixer

Wooden spoon

Cookie sheet

Oven mitts

Plastic wrap

Aluminum foil

3 cups sugar

¼ teaspoon salt

7 tablespoons powdered cocoa

One 12-ounce can evaporated milk

1 teaspoon vanilla extract

4 eggs, beaten

1 stick butter, melted

2 cups flaked coconut

1 cup chopped pecans

Two 9-inch unbaked pie shells

1. Preheat the oven to 350 degrees.

2. In a large bowl, place the sugar, salt, powdered cocoa, evaporated milk, vanilla extract, eggs, and melted butter. Mix with an electric mixer until smooth. Stir in the coconut and chopped pecans. Divide the batter evenly between the two pie shells. Place the pies on a cookie sheet.

3. Bake for 40 minutes, or until the pies are set in the middle. Have an adult help you remove the pies, and allow them to cool completely. Cover with a layer of plastic wrap and then wrap again with aluminum foil. Keep refrigerated until ready to slice. You can cut the pie at the bake sale, or cut it at home and wrap each piece individually in plastic wrap.

Makes 2 pies, 8 slices each, for a total of 16 slices. Pie is very rich!

$1.00 a piece

Cupcakes

No one can resist a cupcake!

2 muffin pans

24 paper cupcake liners

Liquid measuring cup

Large bowl

Electric mixer

Rubber spatula

Oven mitts

Wire racks

Dry measuring cups

Measuring spoons

Medium bowl

Butter knife

One 18¼-ounce package cake mix, any flavor

1 stick butter, at room temperature

3 eggs

2 cups confectioners' sugar, sifted

3 tablespoons butter, at room temperature

1 teaspoon vanilla extract

1 tablespoon milk (or more, if needed)

Sprinkles, colored sugar, or edible cake decorations

1. Preheat the oven to 350 degrees. Place paper cupcake liners in 24 baking cups of muffin pans.

2. Place cake mix, 1¼ cups water, 1 stick butter, and eggs in a large bowl, and mix with an electric mixer until batter is very smooth. Scrape down sides of the bowl with a rubber spatula and mix again. Fill each cupcake liner a little more than half full.

3. Bake cupcakes in the middle of the oven for 20 to 24 minutes. Do not overbake. Have an adult help you remove the cupcakes from the oven, and allow the cupcakes to cool for about 5 minutes. Remove cupcakes, in liners, and place onto wire racks, and allow them to cool completely before icing.

4. To make icing, place confectioners' sugar, 3 tablespoons butter, vanilla extract, and milk into a medium bowl, and mix with an electric mixer until smooth. Add a little more milk if icing is not easy to spread.

5. Using a butter knife, spread a thin layer of icing on each cupcake. Decorate with sprinkles, colored sugar, or edible decorations purchased in the cake-decorating section of a grocery store or specialty store.

Makes 24 cupcakes

CHAPTER THREE

Pool Party

Pool parties are usually held when it's hot. And Savannah's tropical climate always makes me think of Mexican food. It looks so pretty, and tastes so good when you're hungry—and swimming sure makes you hungry! The Mexican theme also lends itself to easy, colorful decorations and making the most out of summertime ingredients like tomatoes and fruit. This is a terrific menu for your vegetarian friends, as there is no meat in anything except the taquito casserole.

Be sure to have some beach balls, foam footballs, floats, and big inner tubes available. You could even get some of those little squirt guns at the dollar store for some added fun. Remind your adult chaperones to have a first-aid kit handy in the event there are bumps or bruises from horsing around! Be safe always, please.

My suggestion is to set up the food inside to keep the bugs away. If you've got a screened-in area, that's perfect, because your buddies can eat in their suits and drip to their hearts' content. It goes without saying that you need plenty of waterproof seating.

Let the party develop for an hour or so, then bring out the spread and ring a bell to let everyone know the food is available. These recipes are just beautiful because of the many colors of the ingredients, and would look good in brightly colored solid bowls or even wooden bowls. Let your guests eat at will!

We've saved one recipe to be cooked *at* the party! Cooking in front of your guests is a great way to entertain!

Pool Party Manners

- Be sure to notify your neighbors about your party so they will be prepared for the music, traffic, and noise, if that might be an issue.
- Even though you want everyone to have fun, post the pool safety rules—no running, pushing, or holding someone underwater. No spitting or blowing your nose in the water, either! There should never be any glass around the pool area.
- Anticipate your guests' needs—extra towels, food and drink, utensils and napkins, and bathroom facilities. If at all possible, use cloth napkins or heavy paper towels. Paper napkins don't work at a pool party because of all the water!

Cooking Lesson

Some dishes actually are better when made up in advance, and others don't hold up so well. The Black Bean and Corn Salsa is actually better the second day, but add the cilantro just before the party starts to give the salsa a fresh pop. The Fruit Salsa, however, has to be made the morning of the party. Finely diced fruit can take on a brownish color, which is why I add the limeade. Don't overbake a casserole with cheese on it. The cheese is perfect one minute, and brown and crusty the next. Be sure to set the timer on all baked goods!

Black Bean and Corn Salsa

This is delicious, and actually tastes better the day after it's made. Add the cilantro at the last minute, however, so it will have that delicious, grassy pop.

Large bowl

Wooden spoon

Small bowl

Measuring spoons

Whisk

Two 14-ounce cans black beans, rinsed and drained

One 10-ounce package frozen niblet corn, uncooked and thawed

4 Roma tomatoes, diced

½ green pepper, finely diced

½ red onion, finely diced

2 cloves garlic, minced

Juice of 2 limes

1 tablespoon balsamic vinegar

1 tablespoon extra-virgin olive oil

1 teaspoon cumin

1 teaspoon Creole seasoning

½ teaspoon salt

2 teaspoons Texas Pete hot sauce

3 tablespoons fresh cilantro, finely minced

1. Stir together the beans, corn, tomatoes, green pepper, onion, and garlic in a large bowl.

2. In a small bowl, combine the lime juice, vinegar, olive oil, cumin, Creole seasoning, salt, and hot sauce. Whisk. Pour over black bean mixture and stir gently. Refrigerate. When ready to serve, stir in the fresh cilantro. Serve with tortilla chips or corn chips.

Makes about 4 cups, which will serve about 12 guests

Fruit Salsa with Cinnamon Tortilla Chips

Sweet fruit and cinnamon tortilla chips—how could you go wrong?

Cutting board

Medium, sharp knife or Food processor

Medium bowl

Wooden spoon

Measuring spoons

Pastry brush

Kitchen shears or Pizza cutter

Cookie sheet

Oven mitts

1 pound strawberries, washed and stems removed

2 Golden Delicious apples, peeled and quartered

2 kiwis, peeled

1 tablespoon sugar

1 tablespoon brown sugar

1 tablespoon frozen limeade concentrate (use the rest to make a pitcher of limeade)

1 package 8-inch flour tortillas

Cinnamon sugar

1. Preheat the oven to 350 degrees.

2. With the assistance of an adult, finely chop the strawberries, apples, and kiwis by hand with a cutting board and a sharp knife, or chop each fruit individually in a food processor. Finely chop, but do not puree, so be sure to use the pulse button.

3. Place the fruit in a medium bowl. Stir in the sugar, brown sugar, and limeade concentrate. Cover and keep refrigerated until ready to serve, no more than 4 hours.

4. Lightly brush each flour tortilla with a little water, then use a pair of kitchen shears or a pizza cutter to cut each tortilla into eighths. Sprinkle the tortilla pieces with cinnamon sugar. Place the tortilla pieces on a cookie sheet, and bake for 10 minutes, until crisp. Have an adult help you remove the tortillas from the oven, and allow them to cool. Serve the cinnamon tortillas with the salsa. Tortilla chips can be made in advance and stored in a plastic freezer bag.

Makes about 3 cups, which will serve about 12 guests

Fresh Salsa

This is way better than the kind that comes in a jar.

Large bowl   Measuring spoons   Wooden spoon   3 large, ripe tomatoes, diced

One 4-ounce can chopped green chilies   1 clove garlic, minced or pressed   1 small onion, finely chopped   1 jalapeño pepper, seeded, deveined, and chopped

(Get an adult to do this for you, if possible. If not, wear thin plastic gloves to do this. Throw the seeds away, and then remove the gloves and discard. If any juice or seed residue gets on your fingers, and then you rub your eyes or nose, it will burn for hours!)

1 small green or red pepper, finely chopped   1 tablespoon olive oil   2 tablespoons red wine vinegar

Combine all of the ingredients and stir them together with a spoon in a large bowl. Cover the container and chill the salsa. Serve with plain tortilla chips.

Serves 12 guests

Taquito Enchiladas

*Taquitos are popular in Mexico. Serve them with all the condiments,
and it's like having a taco with a salad on top.*

9-by-13-inch
baking dish

Dry measuring
cups

Plastic wrap

Aluminum foil

5 small
bowls

Cooking
spray

Frozen
chicken
taquitos—
about 2 per
guest

One 19-ounce
can green or
red enchilada
sauce for every
16 taquitos

2 cups grated
Mexican-
blend cheese
for every 16
taquitos

One 2-ounce
can black olives
for every 16
taquitos

1 small head
romaine
lettuce,
shredded,
for every 16
taquitos

2 large tomatoes,
finely chopped,
for every 16
taquitos

1 cup sour
cream for
every 16
taquitos

One 16-ounce
jar mild salsa for
every 16 taquitos

1. Spray a 9-by-13-inch baking dish with cooking spray. Place frozen taquitos in the baking dish, no more than two deep. Cover with the enchilada sauce. Sprinkle with the cheese. Cover dish with plastic wrap and refrigerate until party time.

2. When ready to bake: Remove the plastic wrap. Preheat the oven to 425 degrees. Bake the casserole for 20 to 25 minutes, until hot and the cheese is bubbly.

3. Have an adult help you remove the casserole from the oven and cover it with foil to keep warm. Remove the foil when you're ready to serve. Have bowls of black olives, lettuce, tomatoes, sour cream, and salsa to put over the taquitos. Make up one plate for your guests, and leave it next to the taquitos as a "model" so your guests will know how to dress up their taquitos. The order is lettuce shreds, tomatoes, sour cream, black olives, and then salsa!

Allow 2 taquitos for small eaters and 3 for bigger ones (usually boys)

Stuffed Chilies

Let your vegetarian friends know that there's no meat in these tasty chilies.

 Paper towels

 Dry measuring cups

 Medium bowl

 Wooden spoon

 Measuring spoons

 9-by-13-inch baking dish

 Oven mitts

 Three 4-ounce cans roasted whole green chilies, peeled (each can contains 3 chilies)

 2 cups grated Monterey Jack cheese

 8 ounces cream cheese, at room temperature

 1 teaspoon cumin

 ½ cup fresh cilantro, finely chopped

 Cooking spray

 1½ cups grated queso blanco or mozzarella cheese

1. Drain the chilies and pat dry. Combine the Monterey Jack cheese and the cream cheese in a medium bowl and stir well with a spoon. Add the cumin and cilantro and stir again.

2. Using a spoon, stuff the peppers with the cheese. Place them side by side in a 9-by-13-inch baking dish that has been sprayed with cooking spray. Sprinkle the queso blanco or mozzarella cheese over the top of the peppers.

3. When ready to cook, preheat the oven to 350 degrees. Place the baking dish in the oven and bake for 30 minutes, until the cheese topping is melted and the cheese filling is bubbling. Have an adult help you remove the dish from the oven. Serve hot. Some guests may want just half a chili as they are rich!

Serves 9

Orangeade

This is a delightful thirst-quencher.

Saucepan

Liquid
measuring cup

2-quart pitcher

Dry measuring cups

2 cups fresh
orange juice

½ cup sugar

4 cups water

Place the orange juice in a 2-quart pitcher. Have an adult help you heat the sugar and water in a saucepan until the sugar has melted. Allow it to cool. Add the cooled water to the orange juice. Refrigerate until serving time. Serve with ice.

Makes about eight 6-ounce servings

Limeade

In parts of Mexico, both lemons and limes are called "lemons." You can make this with either lemons or limes. It's frequently served with Mexican meals.

Saucepan

Liquid
measuring cup

2-quart pitcher

Dry measuring cups

1 cup fresh
lemon or lime
juice

½ cup sugar

6 cups water

Place the lemon or lime juice in a 2-quart pitcher. Have an adult help you heat the sugar and water in a saucepan until the sugar has melted. Allow it to cool. Add the cooled water to the lemon or lime juice. Refrigerate until serving time. Serve with ice.

Makes about nine 6-ounce servings

Sopaipillas with Cinnamon and Sugar

You will have to let an adult do the frying, but you can mix up the dough and shake the hot bread puffs in the cinnamon-sugar mixture. Believe me, your friends will be impressed.

 Dry measuring cups

 Measuring spoons

 Food processor

 Liquid measuring cup

 Plastic wrap

 Resealable plastic bag

Small bowl

 Wooden spoon

 2 brown paper bags

 Butter knife

 Rolling pin

 Pizza cutter

 Electric skillet

 Slotted kitchen spoon

 Paper towels

 2 cups unbleached all-purpose flour

 ½ teaspoon salt

 2 teaspoons baking powder

 1 tablespoon shortening

 ²/₃ cup warm water

 1 cup sugar

 1 tablespoon cinnamon

 Oil for deep-frying

1. Place the flour, salt, and baking powder into the food processor and pulse several times. This will sift the ingredients. Add the shortening and pulse until the mixture is blended. Add the warm water through the food tube, and pulse again until the mixture forms into a ball. Get an adult to help you remove the dough (the blades are sharp!).

2. Wrap the dough in plastic wrap and place it in a plastic bag. Put it in the refrigerator for 24 hours.

3. Mix the sugar and cinnamon in a small bowl, and place it in a double-layered brown paper bag. Do not shake the hot puffs in a plastic bag! They will melt the plastic.

4. When you are ready to cook the sopaipillas, cut the dough in half. On a lightly floured surface, roll out the dough about $\frac{1}{3}$ inch thick. Use a pizza cutter to cut it into 3-inch squares.

5. Set up your cooking station in an out-of-the-way place where no one can accidentally run into the hot pan with hot oil! Heat about 3 inches of oil in an electric skillet set at 400 degrees. Carefully place dough squares into the hot oil and cook until puffed, turning once, until browned on all sides, about 4 to 5 minutes. Drain the sopaipillas on paper towels, then immediately place two at a time in the paper bag filled with the cinnamon-sugar mixture. Shake until they are coated. Place them on a serving dish and let your guests enjoy!

Makes about 25 to 30 sopaipillas

What's

New for Lunch?

There's no way to compete with your mom's leftover spaghetti or lasagna as a lunch favorite. Instead, I'm offering up some fresh ideas that were very popular with my tasters.

The most important part of packing a good school lunch is to keep it safe. Bacteria multiply quickly when a room is warm and there is a source of food and moisture—just the conditions found in your lunch box! So pack one of those freezer gel packs to keep things chilled. Also, be sure to carry one of those small bottles of hand sanitizer and apply right before eating.

As for the food itself, one of the most important things you can pack in your lunch is protein—found in eggs, meat, fish, chicken or turkey, milk, and cheese. That's because protein is brain food—it is metabolized more slowly than carbohydrates, and so it stays with you longer.

Lunch Manners

Manners are all about thinking of others. When you are using the microwave oven in the cafeteria, it is important to think of all those who will come behind you! Always cover your food with a napkin or piece of waxed paper so that it doesn't pop and spew all over the microwave. Throw away your trash so that no one else has to clean up behind you!

Cooking Lesson

Our cooking lesson for this section is really a packing lesson. I always say that you eat with your eyes first, and that's true for school lunch, too. I suggest that you pack everything in resealable plastic bags to keep food from spilling out into your lunch box. Invest in some good plastic storage containers with tight-fitting lids, and make sure you put them in the dishwasher every evening so they will get sanitized before you use them again. If you're a salad lover, have one bowl that is a little larger than you need. Put all of the salad ingredients in the bowl, put the lid on, and shake until everything is mixed.

Mandarin Orange and Feta Salad

This has an Asian-food taste.
You could also add about ¼ cup of chow mein noodles for crunch.

Dry measuring cups

2-cup storage container

Small resealable plastic bags

Liquid measuring cup

Small storage container

Measuring spoons

1 small romaine lettuce heart, chopped into bite-size pieces

¼ cup seasoned almonds

¼ cup crumbled feta cheese

¼ cup chow mein noodles (optional)

One 8-ounce can mandarin oranges, drained

½ cup diced cooked chicken
(use leftover fried, baked, or grilled chicken)

⅓ cup Briannas Ginger Mandarin Salad Dressing*

1. Measure 1½ cups of the romaine into a 2-cup container with a tight-fitting lid. Place the almonds, feta cheese, and chow mein noodles, if using, on top of the romaine and put the lid on the container. Place the oranges into a small plastic bag. Place the chicken into another small plastic bag. Place the salad dressing into another small container with a tight-fitting lid.

2. At lunchtime, add the oranges and the chicken to the 2-cup container. Pour on the dressing, put the lid on the container, and toss until all of the ingredients are combined.

Serves 1

*If you cannot find the recommended dressing, make your own:

Soy Salad Dressing

1 cup vegetable oil

⅓ cup sugar

½ cup rice wine vinegar

1 tablespoon soy sauce

Place in a jar with a tight lid and shake. Store in refrigerator. Bring to room temperature and shake well before using.

Pasta Primavera

This is yummy right after you prepare it, and just as yummy reheated.

Medium
pot

Measuring
spoons

Kitchen
fork

Dry measuring cups

Colander

Small skillet

Wooden spoon

Liquid
measuring cup

1 teaspoon
salt

4 ounces fettuccine

⅓ cup broccoli florets
(the little treelike pieces of
broccoli that you break off)

5 tablespoons
butter

1 clove garlic,
crushed and minced

1 cup sliced fresh
mushrooms (optional)

One 4-ounce can
cooked carrots, drained

½ cup
half-and-half

½ cup chicken
broth

¾ cup shredded
Parmesan cheese

1. Fill a medium pot with water and add the salt. Bring the water to a boil, break the fettuccine into the pot, and cook the noodles until they are tender, about 10 minutes. Stir several times with a kitchen fork to keep the noodles from sticking together. For the last 2 minutes, add the broccoli florets to the water and let them boil with the noodles. Let an adult help you drain the noodles and broccoli. Leave them in the colander while you make the sauce. Do not wash the pot.

2. In a small skillet, melt 1 tablespoon butter. Add the garlic and the mushrooms, if using, and sauté until the mushrooms are soft, about 3 minutes. Stir in the carrots.

3. In the pot that you cooked the noodles in, combine 4 tablespoons butter, the half-and-half, and the chicken broth. Cook over low heat until the butter melts completely. Add ½ cup Parmesan cheese and stir until the mixture is smooth. Turn off the heat. Add the vegetables and the fettuccine to the sauce and stir with the fork until everything is combined.

4. Allow to cool. Refrigerate in a covered container. Take about 1½ cups of the pasta primavera to school in a microwave-safe container with a tight-fitting lid. Take the remaining ¼ cup shredded Parmesan in a plastic bag. When ready to eat, remove the lid and microwave the fettuccine on high for 90 seconds (be sure to cover the top with a piece of waxed paper). Stir to combine. Sprinkle the Parmesan cheese on top.

Makes three 1½-cup servings

Cheeseburger Casserole

This tastes like a cheeseburger without the bun.

Large skillet

Wooden spoon

Measuring spoons

Medium pot

Colander

9-by-13-inch baking dish

Dry measuring cups

1 pound ground beef

1 large onion, choppe
(you might want to leave t
out if you don't like onior
breath at school)

1 green pepper, chopped

One 28-ounce can chopped tomatoes, with juice

1 tablespoon Worcestershire sauce

1 teaspoon dried oregano

1½ teaspoons salt

½ teaspoon pepper

8 ounces wide egg noodles

Cooking spray

2 cups grated sharp Cheddar cheese

1. Preheat the oven to 350 degrees. In a large skillet, cook the ground beef over medium heat, stirring to break up the lumps, until all of the pink is gone from the meat. Get an adult to help you drain off the fat. Add the onion and the green pepper, and cook until the vegetables are tender, about 5 minutes. Add the tomatoes, with juice, and the Worcestershire sauce, oregano, 1/2 teaspoon salt, and pepper. Bring to a boil, then lower the heat to low. Simmer the mixture for about 15 minutes.

2. Fill medium pot half full of water. Add 1 teaspoon salt. Bring the water to a boil. Stir in the noodles and boil for about 8 minutes, until tender. Get an adult to help you drain the noodles. Return the noodles to the pot. Pour the tomato mixture over the noodles and stir until blended.

3. Put the noodle mixture into a baking dish that you have sprayed with cooking spray. Top with cheese. Bake for about 15 minutes, until the cheese is melted. Enjoy it as a family meal, then refrigerate the leftovers.

4. Take leftovers to school in a small microwave-safe container with a tight-fitting lid. Before heating, unsnap the lid to allow steam to escape. Heat casserole in the microwave oven for about 90 seconds.

Serves 6

Chicken Caesar Wrap

This tastes just like the wraps you get at the deli.

Dry measuring cups

Resealable plastic bag

Liquid measuring cup

Small storage container

Waxed paper

⅓ cup chopped romaine lettuce

⅓ cup chopped cooked chicken breast

(can use baked chicken, canned chicken, fried chicken strips, etc.)

⅓ cup shredded Parmesan cheese

⅓ cup Newman's Own Caesar salad dressing

1 tomato or spinach whole-grain wrap

1. Combine the romaine lettuce, chicken breast, and Parmesan cheese in a plastic bag. Put the salad dressing in a small container with a tight-fitting lid. Roll the wrap up in a large piece of waxed paper. Place them all in your lunch box.

2. At lunchtime, combine the salad dressing and the lettuce mixture in the plastic bag. Close the top and shake well to mix. Unroll the wrap and place the chicken salad on the wrap. Fold in each side of the wrap, then roll up the wrap tightly. Enjoy!

3. You can also prepare the sandwich at home. Combine the romaine, chicken breast, Parmesan, and dressing in a small bowl. Mix well. Place in the center of the wrap. Fold in each side of the wrap, then roll up tightly. Cut in half for easier eating. Wrap each half in plastic wrap.

Makes 1 wrap

Roast Beef and Cheddar Wrap

Roast beef and Cheddar is a winning combination.

Resealable
plastic bag

Butter knife

Measuring
spoons

Waxed
paper

2 slices roast
beef

2 tablespoons
shredded Cheddar
cheese

1 tablespoon
mayonnaise

1 tomato or spinach
whole-grain wrap

1. Combine the roast beef and the Cheddar cheese in a plastic bag. Using a butter knife, spread the mayonnaise on half of the wrap and roll it up in a large piece of waxed paper. Place them in your lunch box.

2. At lunchtime, unroll the wrap and place the roast beef and Cheddar mixture on the wrap. Fold up each side of the wrap, then roll it up tightly. Enjoy!

Makes 1 wrap

Barbecue Tuna Sandwich

This is full of protein and is very low in fat. It dates back to my Bag Lady days.

Measuring spoons

Small bowl

Spoon

Plastic wrap

One 6-ounce can chunk light tuna in water, drained

2 tablespoons favorite barbecue sauce

1 whole wheat bun

Combine the tuna and barbecue sauce in a small bowl. Stir gently with a spoon until mixed. Spoon about half of the mixture onto a whole wheat bun. Wrap tightly in plastic wrap.

Serves 1

Crustless Spinach Cheese Quiche

This is packed with vitamins and protein, but is meatless—perfect if you're a vegetarian.

Plate

Medium bowl

Dry measuring cups

Measuring spoons

Blender *or* Food processor

Wooden spoon

9-by-13-inch baking dish

Oven mitts

One 10-ounce package frozen chopped spinach

4 eggs

1 cup sour cream

1 cup small-curd cottage cheese

½ cup grated Parmesan cheese

4 tablespoons unbleached all-purpose flour

1 teaspoon salt

¼ teaspoon pepper

2 cups grated Cheddar cheese

Cooking spray

1. Preheat the oven to 325 degrees. Unwrap the spinach and place it, box and all, on a plate. Place in the microwave and cook on high power for 4 minutes. Allow it to cool, then squeeze out all of the liquid. Place the spinach in a medium bowl.

2. Get an adult helper to assist you in placing the eggs, sour cream, cottage cheese, Parmesan cheese, flour, salt, and pepper into a blender or food processor. Blend for about 1 minute, until the mixture is smooth.

3. Pour the mixture into the bowl with the spinach. Add the Cheddar cheese. Blend with a spoon until well mixed.

4. Spray a 9-by-13-inch baking dish with cooking spray. Pour the spinach mixture into the baking dish and smooth out the top with the back of the wooden spoon.

5. Bake for 45 minutes, until set. Get an adult to help you remove it from the oven. It will be puffed up when you first take it out, then it will fall slightly as it stands. Allow it to cool, then keep it refrigerated.

6. Cut it into squares and carry one to school in a microwave-safe storage container with a tight-fitting lid. At lunchtime, lift the lid so that the steam can come out, and microwave the quiche on high power for about 90 seconds.

Makes about 8 servings

CHAPTER FIVE

A

Sleepover

Inviting your friends over to your house to spend the night is so much fun . . . late nights, long talks, and lost sleep can make for lasting friendships. Of course, delicious food that you can prepare yourself makes the whole event even more special. How about a fondue party?

Fondue parties were all the rage when I was much, much younger, and they were and still are a great way to laugh while you cook and eat, and you know how much I like to do all three of those things! It's the one time when it's okay not only to put your *elbows* on the table, but to lean your *whole body* on the table!

You may be able to find fondue pots at garage sales, but if not, they are back in style and available everywhere housewares are sold. You usually make cheese fondue or chocolate fondue in a ceramic pot, which keeps the food at a low temperature so it doesn't scorch. The heat can be electric or from a Sterno, which you can also buy from most grocery stores and housewares departments. Read the directions carefully if you are using either type of pot. A third type of fondue is hot-oil fondue, in which you fry all sorts of delicious things, like seafood, beef or chicken, or mushrooms. However, I do not recommend that you attempt this type of fondue, even with an adult helper. Hot oil is just too dangerous! So I've included recipes only for cheese and chocolate fondue.

Here are some tips for a successful fondue party:

- Have plates, forks, knives, and napkins already laid out for everyone.
- Serve a specialty iced tea or sparkling apple juice to drink.
- Most pots come with four skewers, and I'm thinking that's enough company for a sleepover.
- Demonstrate how to dip your fork into the food and scrape it off onto the plate. Skewers *cannot* go into your mouth, for safety's sake. If someone forgets and puts a skewer into his/her mouth, wash it immediately. Skewers shouldn't go back into the pot after they've been in your mouth, to prevent germs from being "cooked" along with your food!
- The chunks of food need to be about 1 inch square. Small chunks will fall from your skewer into the pot when they are weighed down with the sauce.

Fondue Manners

- Once you dip your food in the pot, hold it over the pot until the cheese or chocolate stops dripping, then put the food on your plate to eat it.
- Don't put your skewer in your mouth! It's got to go back in the pot! (See page 99.)
- If you have long hair, you must tie it back so that it doesn't get in the food, or in the Sterno!
- For safety reasons, no horseplay! All that dipping makes for fun conversation, but safety always comes before fun.
- Be sure you clean up when you're done!

Cooking Lesson

When cooking cheese or chocolate, low heat is the key. When cheese is cooked at a high temperature, it becomes hard and brittle. When chocolate is cooked at a high temperature, it can become scorched. You can't "fix" cheese or chocolate once you've ruined it. So be patient and cook at the lowest heat possible! You can also melt both cheese and chocolate in the microwave. Again, gentleness is the key. Put the cheese or chocolate in a microwave-safe bowl and cook it for 1 minute at high power. Stir. If it is not quite melted, microwave it for 30 seconds more and check again. This is almost always enough heat to melt about 2 cups of cheese or chocolate.

I suggest you purchase or prepare fried chicken strips for your main course. The cheese fondue will have two vegetables and bread, and the chocolate fondue has two fruits and either angel food cake or pound cake. You'll have all of the food groups covered if you add a simple protein to balance out the dinner.

I've also provided you the recipes for your breakfast for the next morning. You'll want to prepare those dishes in advance so you can sleep in with your friends while breakfast is cooking!

The recipes serve at least eight—four sleepover guests and the rest of the family!

Basic Cheese Fondue

*The classic cheese fondue is Swiss cheese and white wine.
I switched to Cheddar, and it's just delicious!*

 2 platters

 2 medium glass bowls

 Waxed paper

 Oven mitts

 Tongs

 Low-temperature fondue pot (electric or Sterno), with skewers

 Dry measuring cups

 Measuring spoons

 Wooden spoon

 1 loaf sourdough or French bread, cut into big bite-size cubes

 2 stalks broccoli, broken into big bite-size florets

 1 small head cauliflower, broken into big bite-size florets

 1 clove garlic, peeled

 2 cups grated Cheddar cheese

 4 ounces cream cheese (cut an 8-ounce block in half)

 ½ cup sour cream

 One 5-ounce can evaporated milk

 1 tablespoon lemon juice

 ½ teaspoon salt

 ¼ teaspoon pepper

 ¼ teaspoon paprika

1. Put the bread cubes onto a platter. Put the broccoli florets into a medium glass bowl, rinse the florets, and drain, leaving just a little water in the bowl. Cover with waxed paper and microwave on high for 3 minutes, until steaming and tender-crisp. Do the same thing with the cauliflower. Let an adult help you remove the bowls from the microwave; the steam will be hot! Use tongs to place the vegetables on a separate platter or plate. You do not want any of the liquid from the vegetables.

2. Rub the inside of the fondue pot with the garlic clove. Throw the clove into the pot. Add the cheese, cream cheese, sour cream, evaporated milk, and lemon juice. Have an adult light the sterno or turn the electric pot on low. Stir with a wooden spoon until all of the cheese is melted and the mixture is smooth. Add the salt, pepper, and paprika. Stir again.

3. Place a piece of bread, broccoli, or cauliflower onto a skewer and dip it into the cheese, hold it over the pot until the excess drips off, and then place the cheese-coated bread, broccoli, or cauliflower on your plate. Enjoy!

4. Discard any leftover dip. It may contain bacteria from all of the dipping.

Serves 8

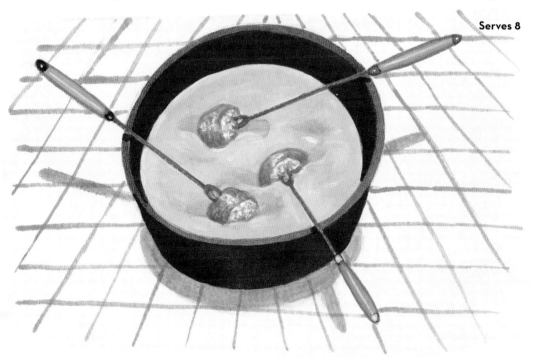

Chocolate Dessert Fondue

Chocolate sauce doesn't get any easier than this!

Low-temperature fondue pot (electric or Sterno), with skewers

Measuring spoons

Wooden spoon

One 12-ounce package semisweet chocolate chips

One 14-ounce can sweetened condensed milk, fat-free or regular

1 teaspoon vanilla extract

1 small pound cake or angel food cake, cut into big bite-size pieces

1 quart strawberries, washed and stems removed—leave these whole!

2 bananas, peeled and cut into big bite-size pieces (about 1½ inches long)

1 recipe Peanut Butter Balls (see page 106)

1. Place the chocolate chips and the sweetened condensed milk into the fondue pot. Heat gently until the chocolate is melted. Add vanilla extract. Stir well.

2. Skewer pieces of cake, whole strawberries, slices of banana, and peanut butter balls, and swirl them in the warm chocolate. Place them on your plate to eat.

3. Discard any leftover dip. It may contain bacteria from all of the dipping.

Serves 8

Peanut Butter Balls

*I used to eat these when I was little, and I still love them—
especially dipped in chocolate!*

Dry measuring cups

Small
bowl

Rubber
spatula

Wooden
spoon

Flat storage
container

½ cup creamy
peanut butter

½ cup
honey

⅔ cup nonfat instant
powdered milk

1. Put the peanut butter, honey, and powdered milk into a small bowl. Use the spatula to scrape all of the peanut butter and honey out of the measuring cup. Stir well with a spoon. Allow to chill for 2 hours.

2. Gently shape the peanut butter dough into walnut-size balls in the palms of your hands.

3. Refrigerate the balls in a flat storage container with a lid so that they will get very firm and won't break apart in your fondue pot.

Makes about 1 dozen balls

Sweet-and-Sour Sausages

Want a delicious snack for later in the evening? Try this!

 Dry measuring cups

 Measuring spoons

 Low-temperature fondue pot (electric or Sterno), with skewers

 Wooden spoon

 1½ cups ketchup

 2 tablespoons red wine vinegar

 2 tablespoons soy sauce

 3 tablespoons packed brown sugar

 One 16-ounce package cocktail sausages

1. Place the ketchup, vinegar, soy sauce, and brown sugar into the fondue pot and stir well. Add the sausages and let them cook over very low heat for about 20 minutes, until they are very warm and have absorbed the flavor of the sauce.

2. Use your skewers to spear a sausage, place it on your plate, and enjoy! Be sure to get plenty of the yummy sauce!

3. Discard any leftover sauce, as it may contain bacteria from all of the dipping.

Serves 8

Morning Yogurt Smoothie

This is so good for you, but so tasty you won't care!

Liquid
measuring cup

Measuring
spoons

Blender

1 pint plain or vanilla-
flavored yogurt

3 cups chilled
pineapple juice

1 cup chilled
orange juice

1 whole banana,
peeled

2 tablespoons
sugar

1 teaspoon
vanilla extract

Place all of the ingredients into a blender and whirl until smooth.
Serve immediately.

Makes about eight 6-ounce servings

Ham Strata

This has ham, eggs, and cheese in it—
so it's like an omelet, without all the fuss!

8-inch square
baking dish

Dry measuring cups

Liquid
measuring cup

Measuring
spoons

Whisk

Butter knife

Plastic wrap

Aluminum foil

Oven mitts

About 3
tablespoons
butter

8 slices
white bread,
with crust

1 cup grated
sharp Cheddar
cheese

1 cup finely
diced ham, any
type you have

1 cup
whole milk

4 eggs

½ teaspoon
salt

½ teaspoon
Dijon mustard

1. Butter an 8-inch square baking dish with about 1 tablespoon of butter.

2. Lay 4 pieces of the bread in the bottom of the pan, side by side. Sprinkle with half of the grated sharp Cheddar cheese. Evenly sprinkle the ham over the cheese. Lay 4 more slices of bread on top of the ham. Sprinkle with the remaining Cheddar cheese.

3. In a large liquid measuring cup, measure the milk. Add the eggs, salt, and mustard. Whisk to combine.

4. Pour the egg mixture over the cheese. Dot with the remaining butter, making sure you put little dots all over the casserole. Cover with plastic wrap and then with aluminum foil. Refrigerate overnight.

5. The next morning, remove the casserole from the refrigerator and allow it to sit out for 30 minutes. While the casserole is sitting out, preheat the oven to 350 degrees.

6. Remove the foil and the plastic wrap, and place the casserole in the oven. Bake for 20 to 25 minutes, until puffed and firm. Have an adult help you remove it from the oven.

7. Cut into small squares to serve.

Serves 8

Breakfast Cheesecake

This is so easy and so delicious!
The secret ingredient is the crescent dinner rolls!

9-by-13-inch
baking dish

Medium
bowl

Dry measuring cups

Measuring
spoons

Electric mixer

Rubber
spatula

2 small
bowls

Waxed
paper

Oven
mitts

Spoon

Plastic wrap

Aluminum foil

Butter knife

Cooking
spray

2 cans 8-count
crescent dinner rolls

16 ounces cream cheese,
at room temperature

1½ cups
sugar

1 teaspoon
vanilla extract

1 stick
butter

2 teaspoons
cinnamon

1. Spray a 9-by-13-inch baking dish with cooking spray. Open one can of dinner rolls. Lay the dinner rolls in the bottom of the baking dish so that they make one large rectangle.

2. In a medium bowl, combine the cream cheese, 1 cup sugar, and vanilla. Mix well with an electric mixer, about 2 minutes.

3. Using a rubber spatula, spread the cream cheese mixture on top of the dinner rolls.

4. Open the second can of dinner rolls. Lay them over the cream cheese so that they make one large rectangle.

5. Melt the butter in a small microwave-safe bowl covered with waxed paper for 30 seconds in the microwave. Have an adult help you remove the bowl and pour the melted butter evenly over the top of the casserole. In another small bowl, mix ½ cup sugar and the cinnamon with a spoon. Using the spoon, sprinkle the cinnamon sugar evenly over the top of the casserole.

6. Cover with plastic wrap and then with aluminum foil. Refrigerate overnight.

7. The next morning, remove the casserole from the refrigerator and allow it to sit out for 30 minutes. Preheat the oven to 350 degrees.

8. Remove the foil and the plastic wrap, and place the casserole in the oven. Bake for 30 to 35 minutes, until puffed and firm. Have an adult help you remove it from the oven. Allow it to sit for 15 minutes before serving.

9. Cut into small rectangles to serve.

Serves 8 to 10

CHAPTER SIX

The Family

Cooking Night

I can't take credit for this idea, but I can tell you how much I like it. One day while watching television, I saw a mother and her children being interviewed about having a once-a-week Family Cooking Night. On Sunday evening, the family sat down and planned the meal, which was usually cooked the following Friday night. They shopped for groceries together and then cooked the meal together. Well, I just thought that was the greatest idea, and so I wanted to share it with you. At a time when parents and children just don't seem to have time to talk to one another, having a night set aside to do two of my favorite things—cooking and eating—just seems like a concept whose time has come!

Here's a nice little menu to get you started, and it stars everybody's favorites—chicken, green beans, and macaroni and cheese! The meal is polished off with banana pudding. Can you imagine a better menu to inspire family togetherness?

Family Cooking Night Manners

Since this is my favorite event in the book, I want you to use your best manners. You know, we always seem to save our manners for people we hardly know, instead of using our best manners for the ones we love the most—our family. This is the night to say "please" and "thank you" and "excuse me." Any young man who holds the chair for his mother or grandmother while she's being seated, and rises from his chair when she leaves the table, scores extra points with me! That's what I always taught Jamie and Bobby, and I'm proud to say that they still remember!

Cooking Lesson

Pan-frying is like sautéing, and it is a wonderful technique for cooking thin pieces of chicken, pork, steak, or fish. You can also sauté shrimp, and vegetables that have been cut into small pieces. In the recipe for Pan-Fried Chicken, you will pan-fry in a mixture of butter and vegetable oil. The butter gives the food a yummy flavor, and the oil helps keep the butter from burning before your food is ready. Always get an adult to help you pan-fry, which is why I've picked this particular recipe for this particular event—because your family is supposed to be involved. Put the butter and oil in a flat-bottomed pan and let the butter melt, then whisk them together, and then add your food. When you are sautéing chicken breasts and fish, turn them only one time. When you are pan-frying small pieces of meat or vegetables, you stir them around in the pan until they are all about the same degree of doneness. Always turn off the heat immediately when the food seems ready. You can always cook it a little more, but you can't take it back once you've gone too far!

Pan-Fried Chicken

Chicken cutlets are chicken breasts sliced in half crosswise, so that the pieces are very thin—less than half an inch. They cook very fast and are just the right amount for most eaters. Big eaters will need two. If you can't find them in the grocery store, get your mom or dad or grandparents to slice chicken breasts into cutlets for you.

Small glass bowl

Paper towels

Dry measuring cups

Pie plate

Dinner plate

Measuring spoons

Large skillet

Whisk

Tongs

2 tablespoons butter

8 chicken cutlets

⅓ cup seasoned bread crumbs

⅓ cup Parmesan cheese

1 tablespoon canola oil

1. Melt 1 tablespoon of butter in a small glass bowl in the microwave. Rinse the chicken and pat it dry. Combine the bread crumbs and the cheese in a small, flat dish, like a pie plate. Swipe the chicken through the butter, and then roll it in the bread crumb mixture. Lay each piece of coated chicken on a dinner plate while you coat all of the cutlets.

2. Put the remaining 1 tablespoon of butter and the oil into the skillet and turn the heat to medium. When the butter is melted, have an adult help you swirl the butter and oil together with a whisk. Using tongs, put the chicken into the pan, and pan-fry about 3 minutes on each side, until the chicken is brown and crusty and cooked through. Do not overcook, or it will be tough.

Serves 6 to 8

Green Beans

My seventh-grade tester said these were the best green beans he'd ever had!

Colander

Medium
pot

Liquid
measuring cup

Measuring
spoons

2 pounds
green beans

2 cups
chicken broth

2 teaspoons House
Seasoning
(see page 124)

1 tablespoon bacon
grease (optional)

1. Snap the ends off the beans. (This is a great job for little brothers or sisters.) Wash the beans and drain them in a colander.

2. Place the beans in a medium pot. Pour in the broth. Measure the House Seasoning and add that to the beans. Add the bacon grease, if using. Turn up the heat and bring the broth to a boil, then reduce the heat to low, place the lid on the pot, and allow the beans to cook for 25 minutes, until tender. Southerners like their beans soft. If you want yours with some crunch, only cook them for 15 minutes.

Serves 8

House Seasoning

I use this at home and in the restaurant on just about everything that's savory!

Dry measuring cups

Small bowl

Spoon

Small storage container

1 cup salt

¼ cup pepper

¼ cup garlic powder

Mix salt, pepper, and garlic powder with a spoon in a small bowl. Store in an airtight container so you can shake it up before measuring. This is very good on most vegetables.

Makes 1½ cups

Three-Cheese Macaroni

This is just great with ham or steak or hamburgers. It also makes a great leftover to take to school in your lunch box.

9-by-13-inch baking dish

Dry measuring cups

Medium pot

Measuring spoons

Wooden spoon

Colander

Medium bowl

Liquid measuring cup

Whisk

Cooking spray

2 cups macaroni

1½ teaspoons salt

2 cups grated sharp Cheddar cheese

2 cups grated mozzarella cheese

1 cup Cheez Whiz

4 tablespoons butter, melted

1 cup whole milk

3 eggs, beaten

½ teaspoon dry mustard

½ teaspoon pepper

1. Preheat the oven to 350 degrees. Spray a 9-by-13-inch baking dish with cooking spray.

2. Put the macaroni in the pot and fill it about halfway with water. Add 1 teaspoon salt. Bring the water to a boil, and stir the macaroni with a wooden spoon so that it doesn't stick together. Let it boil on medium-high heat until it is tender, about 7 to 8 minutes. Stir several times. Let an adult help you drain the macaroni in a colander.

3. Return the hot macaroni to the pot. In a medium bowl, mix the Cheddar cheese and the mozzarella; remove 1 cup of the mixed cheese for the topping. Put the rest of the cheese into the hot macaroni. Add the Cheez Whiz. Stir to blend. Add the melted butter. Stir again.

4. In a large liquid measuring cup, measure the milk, then add the eggs. Whisk to blend. Add ½ teaspoon salt, mustard, and pepper, and whisk again. Add the egg mixture to the macaroni. Stir with the wooden spoon.

5. Pour the macaroni mixture into the prepared baking dish. Smooth the top with the back of the spoon. Sprinkle the remaining 1 cup of cheese evenly over the top of the macaroni. Bake for 35 to 40 minutes, until browned and bubbly.

Serves 8

Toasted Garlic Bread

Toasting makes your bread taste really special.

Cutting
board

Bread
knife

Small
bowl

Metal
spatula

Butter knife

Large skillet *or*
Electric skillet

1 loaf
French bread

4 tablespoons butter,
at room temperature

1 clove garlic,
minced fine

1. Cut the bread into 1-inch slices. Put the butter into a small bowl. Add the minced garlic and stir with the metal spatula.

2. Use the butter knife to spread the butter mixture on one side of each piece of bread.

3. Toast the bread, butter side down, in a skillet over low heat or in an electric skillet set to 250 degrees. When the bread is brown and toasty, remove and serve with the rest of the meal.

Serves 8

Banana Pudding Dessert

Our young teen testers thought this was delicious!

Large
bowl

Liquid
measuring cup

Electric
mixer

9-by-13-inch baking
dish or other 2-quart
dessert dish

Rubber
spatula

1¼ cups
cold water

One 14-ounce
can sweetened
condensed milk

One 3.4-ounce
package instant
vanilla pudding mix

24 to 32 vanilla
wafers

3 large, firm
bananas, sliced

2 cups frozen
whipped
topping, thawed

1. In a large bowl, combine the water, condensed milk, and pudding mix, and beat with an electric mixer on low speed for 2 minutes. Chill for 5 minutes.

2. In the baking dish, make a complete layer of wafers. Cover that layer with about half of the banana slices. Cover the bananas with half of the pudding mixture. Repeat the layers, ending with the pudding. Cover the pudding layer with the whipped topping. Chill until ready to serve.

Serves 8

CHAPTER SEVEN

Christmas Cooking Party

When my boys were little, I used to make food gifts for their teachers. Not only did the teachers love them, but the boys loved the idea that their gifts had been hand-made by their mother! They would always deliver those gifts with a big smile and a sense of pride.

So, why don't you invite a few good friends over for the day for a cooking party? Split the cost of the supplies, and make and package your own Christmas gifts. A Saturday morning is the perfect time for this. Then on Sunday afternoon, make your deliveries to the neighbors, and on Monday morning, take your items to school that have been made for teachers and other special people.

Let's talk about the packaging, which is almost as important as the food gift inside. The best time to purchase small tins for gift giving is during the after-Christmas sales, so if you don't want to get up early the day after Christmas, maybe you can talk an adult into looking for small tins for you. The tins are best for delicate items, like the Stained-Glass Cookies. The Turtles and the Oreo Truffles are sturdy enough to put into a resealable plastic bag. Then you can slip the plastic bag down into a decorative holiday bag that closes with ribbon or a twist tie. Breads are always best double-wrapped, first in plastic, then in foil. That way, they can go straight into the freezer if the recipient wants to save them for later. The Pimento Cheese is a particularly good gift for people who can't have sweets—like diabetics or others who say they are watching their calories. Small crocks or small plastic containers with tight-fitting lids are perfect for packing pimento cheese. You do not have to give large amounts of food—three or four turtles or truffles is plenty. It's the thought that counts!

Cooking Party Manners

Getting along with friends when working on a project together is an important skill you will need throughout your life. Carefully choose the friends you will invite to your cooking party. They should be ones who get along well. Involve your friends in deciding which recipes you will prepare. Let everyone have a turn doing the fun stuff, like stirring and kneading. Let your friends do their own packaging—one of them may have a much better idea about how to make the food look pretty than I do. You want each cook's creativity to come out. You don't want to spoil the party by being bossy.

Cooking Lesson

Making yeast bread is so much fun, and it's really not hard. However, you do have to make sure that your water is warm enough to activate the yeast, but not so warm that it kills the yeast. Follow the directions in the Cheese Bread recipe and your bread will be perfect!

Turtles

These look and taste just like the ones you buy in the store! Ideally, the pecan will peek out from the chocolate, looking like little turtle feet underneath a shell.

Cookie
sheet

Waxed
paper

2 medium
glass bowls

Measuring
spoons

2 spoons

Dry measuring cups

Cooking spray

36 to 40
pecan halves

48 packaged caramels,
unwrapped

4 tablespoons
half-and-half

½ teaspoon
vanilla extract

1½ cups semisweet
chocolate chips

2 teaspoons
shortening

1. Cover a cookie sheet with waxed paper. Spray waxed paper with cooking spray. Arrange nuts on waxed paper, flat side down, spaced about 1 inch apart. Use one nut half per piece of candy. In a medium glass bowl, melt the caramels with the half-and-half in the microwave on high power for about 2 minutes. Add vanilla extract and stir until smooth and thoroughly mixed.

2. Using a spoon, drop a little caramel onto the center of each nut. Allow the caramel to cool, about 30 minutes. If you have leftover caramel, do a few more pecan halves.

3. In another medium glass bowl, melt chocolate with shortening in the microwave on high power for 1 minute. Stir. If not completely melted, microwave for 10 seconds more and stir again. Using another spoon, drop a little chocolate over the caramel on each candy. Allow the candies to set for several hours before removing from the waxed paper.

4. Package several turtles in a resealable plastic bag, and then place each bag into a decorative holiday bag. Or package the turtles in small tins lined with waxed paper.

Makes 36 to 40 turtles

Stained-Glass Cookies

These are really pretty, and each one is different!
One big cookie would make a nice treat, or you can give several small ones.

Cookie
sheets

Aluminum
foil

Dry measuring cups

Large
bowl

Electric
mixer

Measuring
spoons

Small
bowl

Sifter

Plastic
wrap

Rolling
pin

Cutting
board

Cookie
cutters

Wide
spatula

Small, sharp
knife

Resealable
plastic bag

Oven
mitts

1 cup
sugar

1 stick butter, at
room temperature

¼ cup
shortening

2
eggs

1 teaspoon
almond extract

2½ cups
unbleached all-
purpose flour

1 teaspoon
baking powder

1 teaspoon
salt

About 5 rolls
Life Savers

1. Preheat the oven to 375 degrees. Line cookie sheets with aluminum foil.

2. Cream the sugar, butter, and shortening in a large bowl with an electric mixer until thoroughly combined. Add the eggs and almond extract and mix again. In a small bowl, sift together the flour, baking powder, and salt. Add it to the butter mixture and mix on very low speed until everything is combined. Wrap the dough in plastic wrap and chill it for 1 hour.

3. Using a rolling pin, roll dough out onto a cutting board dusted with flour. Cut into shapes with cookie cutters. Using a spatula, transfer the cookies to the cookie sheets. Using a small, sharp knife, cut out shapes in the cookies. Or you can have two sizes of the same cookie cutter (like stars) and use the smaller one to cut out a hole in the larger one. You can reroll the dough you remove with the knife.

4. Place the Life Savers in a heavy-duty resealable plastic bag, and leave it open so that the air can escape. Crunch the Life Savers with the rolling pin, just enough to break them into large chunks. Place several chunks in each cutout.

5. Bake cookies for 9 to 11 minutes, until they are lightly browned and the candy is melted. Have an adult help you remove them from the oven, and allow the cookies to sit on the cookie sheets until they are completely cooled and the candy has rehardened.

It is impossible to say how many cookies this makes, as it depends on the size of your cutters. If you were making plain sugar cookies with 2-inch cutters, the recipe would make about 3 dozen cookies.

Oreo Truffles

One of my young fans—Sophie Nicholls of Fredericksburg, Virginia—sent me this recipe. It's delicious, but you do have to allow time for the dough to set up before you dunk the truffles in the dipping chocolate!

Food processor *or*
Large resealable
plastic bag

Rolling
pin

Large
bowl

Wooden
spoon

Plastic
wrap

Medium
glass bowl

Toothpick

Waxed
paper

One 18-ounce
package Oreo
cookies

8 ounces cream cheese,
at room temperature

1 pound dipping chocolate, dark or white
(This is one of those seasonal items available only
during the holidays. I always pick it up as soon as I
see it so that I have some on hand.)

1. Grind the Oreo cookies in a food processor. Add cream cheese and blend until it forms a ball. Let an adult help you remove the dough from the food processor. (If you don't have a food processor, place the cookies in a large resealable plastic bag, leave it open so the air can escape, and crush the cookies with a rolling pin. Then combine the crumbs and cream cheese in a large bowl.) Wrap the dough in plastic wrap and refrigerate for 1 hour.

2. Pinch off enough dough to roll balls about the size of a walnut. Melt the chocolate in a medium glass bowl in the microwave according to the package directions. Using a toothpick, dip balls into melted chocolate, then place on waxed paper to cool.

3. Truffles may be stored in the refrigerator. Give each person about 4 truffles in a small tin lined with waxed paper.

Makes about 40 truffles

Poppy Seed Loaves

Just about everyone loves poppy seed bread.
This one's chock full of those yummy seeds.

| Two 9-by-5-by-3-inch loaf pans | Large bowl | Dry measuring cups | Liquid measuring cup | Electric mixer |

| Rubber spatula | Measuring spoons | Small bowl | Sifter | Oven mitts |

| Butter knife | Wire racks | Cooking spray | Flour to coat pans | 1½ cups sugar |

| ³/₄ cup oil | 2 eggs | 1 teaspoon vanilla extract | 2 teaspoons almond extract |

| 2 cups unbleached all-purpose flour | 1 teaspoon salt | 1 teaspoon baking soda | 1 cup milk | 3 tablespoons poppy seeds |

1. Preheat the oven to 350 degrees. Prepare two 9-by-5-by-3-inch loaf pans by spraying them with cooking spray. Put about 2 teaspoons of flour in each pan, and turn and tap the pan until the bottom and the sides are coated with flour. Tap out excess flour into the trash can.

2. In a large bowl, beat together the sugar and oil with an electric mixer until well mixed, scraping down the sides and the bottom of the bowl with a spatula. Add the eggs and beat again. Add the vanilla and almond extracts and beat until smooth.

3. In a small bowl, sift together the flour, salt, and baking soda. Add it to the batter and beat on a very low speed for about 2 minutes, until the batter is smooth. Add the milk, and beat until smooth, about a minute. Stir in the poppy seeds with the spatula, mixing well.

4. Pour the mixture into the loaf pans. Bake the loaves for 1 hour.

5. Have an adult help you remove the loaves from the oven, and allow them to sit on the counter for 15 minutes. Then take a butter knife and run it along the sides of the loaves so they will come out of the pan. Gently remove them and allow them to cool completely on wire racks.

6. Wrap the loaves in plastic wrap and then in foil. Tie with a bow.

Makes 2 loaves

Cheese Bread

*Baking bread requires patience, which is a good trait to develop in life!
You have to wait on the yeast to cause the bread to rise, and then you
have to wait while your loaves are doubling in size. The smell of this bread
makes this recipe worth all the waiting!*

2 large
bowls

Dry measuring cups

Measuring
spoons

Liquid
measuring cup

Yeast
thermometer

Wooden
spoon

Cutting
board

Kitchen
towel

Cookie
sheet

Oven
mitts

4 to 4½ cups
unbleached all-
purpose flour

2 tablespoons
sugar

1 teaspoon
salt

Two ¼-ounce
packages dry
yeast

1 cup
milk

½ cup
water

8 ounces grated
sharp Cheddar
cheese

Cooking
spray

Butter for rubbing
the tops of the
warm loaves

1. Mix 1½ cups of flour with the sugar, salt, and undissolved yeast in a large bowl. Combine the milk and water in a liquid measuring cup. Heat in the microwave for 1 minute. Stir. Use a yeast thermometer to test the temperature of the liquid. It should be between 120 and 130 degrees. If it is too warm, allow it to cool, then retest. If it is not warm enough, microwave for 10 seconds more and test again. When it is the proper temperature, add the liquid to the dry ingredients. Stir with a wooden spoon until all the dry ingredients are wet. Add the cheese and stir again. Now start adding the remaining flour ½ cup at a time, stirring with the spoon after each addition. The dough will get stiffer and stiffer as you add the flour. Keep adding flour up to 4½ cups, until the dough is not as sticky.

2. Dump the dough out onto a floured cutting board. Push the dough down with the heels of your hands, then flip the dough over. If the dough is sticky, add flour, 1 tablespoon at a time, onto your board. Keep kneading the dough like this for about 5 minutes. You will really feel it in your arms and shoulders. Take turns!

3. Place the dough into a clean large bowl, sprayed with cooking spray. Turn the dough so that all of it is greased. Cover with a clean kitchen towel, and let it rise in a warm place, like next to the stove, until it has doubled in size, about an hour.

4. Remove the dough from the bowl and punch it with your fist. This will make it deflate and is called "punching the dough down." Now divide the dough into six equal pieces. Roll each one into a long rope of the same length—about 14 inches. Take three of the ropes and braid them together. Braid the other three together. Place the braids onto a cookie sheet sprayed with cooking spray. Cover with the kitchen towel and let them rise again, about an hour.

5. Preheat the oven to 375 degrees. Put the loaves in the exact center of oven, and let them bake for 20 to 25 minutes, until the tops sound hollow when you tap them. The tops will be a medium brown, with specks of dark brown from the baked cheese. Have an adult help you remove the loaves from the oven. Rub the tops with a stick of butter. Cool loaves on wire racks.

6. Wrap each loaf in plastic wrap and then in aluminum foil. Tie with a pretty bow. Give them immediately, or freeze. Write on the card that the bread is best when slices are warmed in the microwave for 20 seconds, or you can reheat the whole loaf at 250 degrees for about 10 minutes.

Makes 2 loaves

Lemon-Dill Rice Mix

We are borrowing this from Paula Deen Celebrates! *It makes a nice gift for those grown-ups on your Christmas list who can't eat sweets or bread! It's so easy that even your little brother or sister can help measure.*

Small
bowl

Measuring
spoons

Dry measuring cups

Wooden
spoon

Sandwich-size
resealable plastic bags

1½ teaspoons
dried grated
lemon zest

½ teaspoon
dried minced
onion

2 chicken bouillon cubes,
crushed, *or* 2 teaspoons
granulated chicken bouillon

1 teaspoon
dried dill weed

½ teaspoon
salt

1¼ cups uncooked
white rice

1. Combine all of the ingredients in a small bowl and mix well. Then put the mixture in a sandwich-size resealable plastic bag and write this recipe on a card: Bring 2½ cups water and 1 tablespoon butter to a boil in a 2-quart saucepan. Add the contents of this package. Reduce the heat to low, cover, and simmer for 20 minutes. Makes 3 cups, about 6 servings.

2. Put the plastic bag into a brown paper bag that you have sponge-painted, with the recipe card stapled to the top. Or place the plastic bag into a holiday gift bag and tie with a twist tie, with the recipe card stapled to the top.

Makes enough for one gift

Homemade
Pimento Cheese

Here's another great gift for those folks on your list who can't eat sweets (maybe an older neighbor?). Give this in 1-cup-size plastic containers with matching lids.

Dry measuring cups

Measuring spoons

Food processor

Rubber spatula

2 cups grated sharp Cheddar cheese

One 2-ounce jar pimentos, with juice

¼ cup mayonnaise

¼ teaspoon pepper

1. Put the ingredients into a food processor, and pulse until all of the ingredients are mixed, about six times. Do not puree!

2. Get an adult to help you transfer the pimento cheese into 1-cup-size plastic containers with matching lids. Put a cute holiday card on top. Refrigerate until you are ready to deliver your gift.

Makes about 2 cups, enough for two 1-cup gifts and a little extra for the cook

CHAPTER EIGHT

The Family Picnic Menu

Some of my fondest memories are of family picnics, especially if I got to take along a friend or two to play with. Even when things go wrong—the ants get in the sandwich bag or the wind blows the paper plates down the beach—picnics provide for a special kind of togetherness. You are with your group, on the ground or in lawn chairs, enjoying a spread in the outdoors.

Savannah is a big picnic city because of all the wonderful locations we have to picnic in. Each year, thousands of people gather for a joint picnic in Forsyth Park, a huge city park in the heart of downtown Savannah. People bring tables and chairs and set the table as if they are having a formal dinner party! On Saint Patrick's Day in Savannah, people set up their picnic areas for the day— arriving early in the morning and staying until late in the afternoon to enjoy the parade and the people-watching. Picnics at the beach on Tybee Island, near Savannah, are particularly fun for kids, especially on holidays like July Fourth and Labor Day. But a picnic *anywhere* is fun, so if you can't get your parents to take you somewhere special, just plan an event in your own backyard!

Here's what I like to take along:

- A cooler on wheels
- A large, washable fabric tablecloth or small, washable quilt (my favorite!). Bring along a second or third quilt for afternoon naps!
- Paper plates, paper cups, napkins, serving utensils, a sharp knife
- A plastic bag with a washcloth and hand sanitizer inside
- A trash bag
- Bug spray
- Sunscreen
- A light jacket if there is any chance the temperature will drop (be sure to check the forecast if you are going to some remote area)

- Chairs and a small table for preparing the food are luxuries you may want to consider. They are hard to carry, but they do make the day more fun if you have some grandparents in the group.
- A Frisbee, football, paddle ball set, or some other fun game to play
- Delicious food and drink—and plenty of it!

Picnic Manners

When you are picnicking, it is important to do your part of the setting up and the taking down. Also, once the blanket or tablecloth is spread, no one gets to put their feet or shoes on it! Sit with your feet off of the quilt—this will keep the center area clean for the food. The simplest way to do a picnic is for everyone to get in their places, then have one person pass out the food. When you get up and down, the blanket or tablecloth gets all messed up. So stay put, ask for what you want, and then say "thank you" when you get it. Finally, be sure to take all of your trash and litter with you. We have to take care of our world, and littering is a big no-no for me!

Cooking Lesson

When you are picnicking, it is important to keep food chilled so that bacteria doesn't grow, which could cause people to become sick. (I've mentioned this in the lunch box chapter as well.) Resealable plastic bags and plastic storage containers with tight-fitting lids are a must for keeping the food looking presentable inside the cooler.

There's really nothing better for a picnic than a sandwich, and some of the simplest ones are the best. You don't want your sandwiches to become soggy, so there are some tricks, like making them right before you leave, and draining soggy ingredients—like pineapple and tomato slices—for at least an hour on paper towels.

Deviled Eggs

These are always a hit.

Medium
pot

Paper towels

Butter
knife

Small
bowl

Potato
masher

Measuring
spoons

Spoon

6 eggs

2 tablespoons
mayonnaise

1 teaspoon
mustard

½ teaspoon
salt

¼ teaspoon
pepper

1. Gently place the eggs in a pot large enough to hold the eggs in one layer. Cover with cold water. Bring the water to a rolling boil, then reduce the heat so that the water is just simmering around the eggs. Simmer for 12 minutes. Then turn off the heat and let the eggs sit in the hot water for 20 minutes while you do other things. When the 20 minutes are up, have an adult help you drain off the hot water, then hold the pot under cold water and let it run until the eggs are cool to the touch. Remove the eggs from the water and let them dry on paper towels.

2. Carefully remove the shell from each egg. Then hold each egg under running water to get off any bits of skin or shell. Drain on paper towels.

3. Carefully cut the eggs in half with a butter knife. Carefully remove the yolks and place all the yolks into a small bowl. Mash the yolks with a potato masher. Add the mayonnaise, mustard, salt, and pepper. Stir with a spoon.

4. Using the spoon, carefully stuff each egg half with the yolk mixture.

5. Store the eggs in a deviled-egg dish with a plastic lid. Or you can put two egg halves together and wrap them in plastic wrap. Each guest gets two halves.

Makes 12 deviled eggs

Potato Salad

Potato salad may be one of my favorite dishes of all time.

Vegetable
peeler

Cutting
board

Medium, sharp
knife

Medium
pot

Measuring
spoons

Fork

Colander

Dry measuring cups

Small
bowl

Wooden
spoon

4 baking
potatoes or
8 to 12 new
potatoes

2½
teaspoons
salt

2 ribs
celery

½ green
pepper

4 hard-cooked eggs,
peeled (see directions
on page 155)

¼ cup sweet
salad cubes

½ teaspoon
pepper

1 cup
mayonnaise

1. Get an adult to help you peel the potatoes and dice them into ½-inch cubes, as they are hard to cut and often roll around on the cutting board. I like either baking potatoes or new potatoes in potato salad. If I use new potatoes, I quarter them and leave the skin on. Put the potatoes into a medium pot with water to cover. Add 1 teaspoon salt to the cooking water and boil the potatoes until they are tender, about 15 minutes. Check periodically with a fork—when the fork glides easily through the potatoes, they are done.

2. While the potatoes are cooking, dice the celery, green pepper, and eggs. When the potatoes are cooked, have an adult help you drain them in a colander. Return them to the pot. Add the celery, green pepper, eggs, and sweet salad cubes. Do not stir yet. In a small bowl, add 1½ teaspoons salt and the pepper to the mayonnaise and stir. Then add the mayonnaise mixture to the hot potatoes and stir until everything is well mixed.

3. Store the potato salad in the refrigerator in a plastic bowl with a tight-fitting lid.

Serves 8 to 10

Pineapple-Cheese Sandwiches

These are a childhood favorite.

Paper
towels

Butter
knife

One 15-ounce can sliced
pineapple, drained

16 slices thin white
sandwich bread

Mayonnaise

8 slices sharp
Cheddar cheese

1. Open the pineapple can and place the drained pineapple slices on paper towels to absorb all the moisture, at least an hour.

2. Wash and dry the pineapple can. Use it as you would a biscuit cutter to cut the bread. Slather mayonnaise on one side of each circle of bread. Place one slice of pineapple on a piece of bread, and top with one slice of Cheddar. Top with another slice of bread.

3. Store sandwiches in resealable plastic bags or flat rectangular plastic containers with tight-fitting lids. Use waxed paper to separate the layers of sandwiches. Keep chilled.

Makes 8 sandwiches

Tomato Sandwiches

There simply isn't a better sandwich,
especially if the tomatoes are homegrown.

Cutting
board

Serrated
knife

Paper
towels

Empty
pineapple can

Small
bowl

Dry measuring cups

Measuring
spoons

Spoon

Butter
knife

2 large
tomatoes

16 slices thin
white sandwich
bread

½ cup
mayonnaise

1 teaspoon
seasoned salt

1 tablespoon real
bacon bits

1. Wash and dry the tomatoes. Have an adult help you slice each tomato into 5 slices, each about ¼ inch thick, on a cutting board using a serrated knife. Lay the tomato slices on paper towels to drain for at least 1 hour.

2. Using the clean, dry pineapple can from the previous recipe (see page 159), cut circles out of the bread. In a small bowl, combine the mayonnaise, seasoned salt, and bacon bits. Stir with a spoon until combined. Spread a thin layer of the seasoned mayonnaise on all of the bread circles. Place a tomato on one circle and cover with another circle.

3. Store sandwiches in flat, rectangular plastic containers with tight-fitting lids. Use waxed paper to separate the layers of sandwiches. Keep chilled.

Makes 8 sandwiches

Olive and Cream Cheese Sandwiches

This is something I discovered at the swimming pool when I was just a girl. A friend brought her lunch to the pool and had olive and cream cheese sandwiches, and I was so jealous I went home and made myself one.

Small
bowl

Measuring
spoons

Rubber
spatula

Dry measuring cups

Cutting
board

Small, sharp
knife

Rolling
pin

8 ounces
cream cheese

1 tablespoon
mayonnaise

1 cup green olives
stuffed with pimentos

8 slices white or
whole wheat bread

1. Unwrap the cream cheese and put it in a small bowl. Let it sit out on the counter until it is very soft, at least 1 hour. Add the mayonnaise and stir with a rubber spatula until blended.

2. Put the olives on a cutting board and have an adult help you cut them in half with a small, sharp knife. Add them to the cream cheese and stir with the spatula.

3. Take one slice of bread and roll it flat with a rolling pin. Using the spatula, spread the entire surface of the bread with a thin layer of the olive spread. Roll up the bread like a jelly roll. Repeat with the rest of the bread and olive spread. You can alternate white and whole wheat slices, which looks really pretty. You can also cut these into pinwheels.

4. Store sandwiches in resealable plastic bags or plastic containers with tight-fitting lids. Keep chilled.

Makes 8 sandwiches

Praline Crunch Brownies

*I used to make these brownies in my Bag Lady days.
People just couldn't get enough of them!*

8-by-11-inch
baking dish

Large
bowl

Liquid
measuring cup

Wooden
spoon

Small
bowl

Dry measuring
cups

Oven
mitts

Cooking
spray

One 21-ounce package
Duncan Hines Family-
Style Chewy Fudge
Brownie mix

2
eggs

¼ cup
cold water

½ cup
vegetable oil

1 stick butter, at
room temperature

½ cup
flour

1 cup
chopped nuts

1 cup packed
brown sugar

1. Preheat the oven to 350 degrees. Spray an 8-by-11-inch baking dish with cooking spray.

2. In a large bowl, combine the brownie mix, eggs, water, and vegetable oil. Stir with a wooden spoon for about 50 strokes. Pour the batter into the pan and use the back of the spoon to spread it evenly. Wash the spoon.

3. In a small bowl, stir together the butter, flour, nuts, and brown sugar with the spoon until well mixed. Using your fingers, evenly distribute the topping over the brownies.

4. Bake the brownies for about 27 to 30 minutes, until the topping is bubbly and the brownies appear set. Have an adult help you remove them from the oven.

5. Allow the brownies to cool completely, about an hour, before you cut them into small squares. Store them in a flat, rectangular plastic container with a tight-fitting lid.

Makes 16 brownies

Oatmeal Raisin Cookies

Kids always like these better without the nuts. I like them really big.

Large bowl

Dry measuring cups

Electric mixer

Measuring spoons

Small bowl

Sifter

Liquid measuring cup

Wooden spoon

Tablespoon

Parchment paper

Cookie sheet

Oven mitts

Wide spatula

Wire rack

2 sticks butter, at room temperature

1 cup packed brown sugar

½ cup sugar

2 eggs

1 teaspoon vanilla extract

1½ cups unbleached all-purpose flour

1 teaspoon baking soda

1 teaspoon salt

1 teaspoon cinnamon

2 cups old-fashioned rolled oats, uncooked

½ cup water

1 cup raisins

1. Preheat the oven to 350 degrees.

2. In a large bowl, combine the butter and the sugars and beat with an electric mixer until very creamy. Add the eggs and vanilla extract, and beat again until mixed. In a small bowl, sift together the flour, baking soda, salt, and cinnamon. Add it to the butter mixture. Add the oats, but don't stir.

3. Measure the water in a glass measuring cup and add the raisins, then microwave for 90 seconds. Allow the raisins to sit on the counter for about 10 minutes. Drain the raisins and add them to the mixture. Stir with a wooden spoon until the oats and raisins are mixed into the dough.

4. Drop heaping tablespoons of batter onto a parchment paper–lined cookie sheet. Leave plenty of room for the cookies to spread.

5. Bake for 10 to 12 minutes, until the cookies are cooked in the middle. Have an adult help you remove the cookies from the oven. Cool on the cookie sheet for about 3 minutes before you transfer to a wire rack to cool completely.

6. Store cookies in resealable plastic bags, or in a metal tin to keep cookies from breaking apart.

Makes about 3 to 4 dozen cookies, depending on size

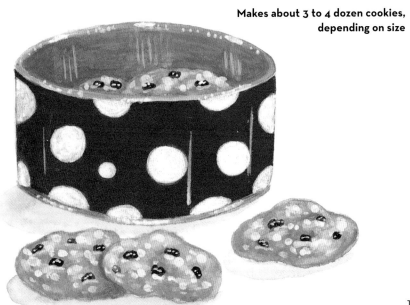

Mother's Day and Father's Day

Cooking has always been a way that I have shown my love for my family—my sons, husband, nieces and nephews, brother, aunts and uncles, and my grandson, Jack. When you prepare food for someone, you are giving them a little something of yourself.

So on Mother's Day or Father's Day, nothing quite says "I love you" like a meal that you cook and serve yourself. If you really want to please your mother and daddy, you will also be sure to clean up the kitchen afterward!

I've got two menu suggestions—one breakfast and one dinner. Whether you are serving breakfast or dinner, make sure that you set the table with pretty place mats, real plates, cloth napkins in napkin rings (these can just be ribbon ties if you don't have real rings), and real glasses.

Here are the two menus:

Breakfast
Sausage and Potato Frittata (a baked omelet)
Popovers
Fresh fruit served with Fruit Dip
Orange juice

Dinner
Bacon-Cheddar Meat Loaf
Garlic Mashed Potatoes
Snap Beans
Drop Biscuits
Black and White Gooey Butter Cake

Sausage and Potato Frittata

This tastes like an egg pie, which it is!

7-inch ovenproof skillet

Wooden spoon

Medium bowl

Dry measuring cups

Measuring spoons

Whisk

Oven mitts

½ pound mild bulk sausage

½ green or red pepper, diced

2 cups frozen hash brown potatoes, thawed

6 eggs

⅓ cup grated Parmesan cheese

⅓ cup shredded sharp Cheddar cheese

1 teaspoon salt

½ teaspoon pepper

1. Position oven rack in the middle of the oven. Preheat the oven to 350 degrees.

2. Use your fingers to crumble the sausage into a 7-inch ovenproof skillet. Sauté the sausage over medium heat until all of the pink is gone, stirring with a wooden spoon to break the sausage apart as it cooks. Add the pepper and allow it to cook in the sausage drippings until tender, about 5 minutes.

3. When the pepper is cooked, have an adult help you drain off any extra fat. Spread the sausage and peppers evenly in the skillet. Take the hash browns and sprinkle them evenly over the sausage.

4. Crack the eggs into a medium bowl. Add the Parmesan, Cheddar, salt, and pepper, and beat well with a whisk. Pour the egg mixture over the sausage and hash browns.

5. Place the skillet in the oven and bake for 18 to 20 minutes, until the center of the frittata is set. Have your adult helper remove the skillet from the oven.

6. Cut frittata into 6 wedges to serve. Best served warm, within about 10 to 15 minutes.

Serves 4 to 6

Popovers

It's amazing to see this runny dough turn into marvelous browned bread!

8 custard cups

Medium bowl with a pouring spout

Liquid measuring cup

Measuring spoons

Electric mixer

Small bowl

Sifter

Dry measuring cups

Rubber spatula

Cookie sheet

Oven mitts

Butter knife

Cooking spray

3 eggs

1 cup milk

3 tablespoons canola oil

1 cup unbleached all-purpose flour

½ teaspoon salt

1. Position oven rack in the middle of the oven. Preheat the oven to 400 degrees. Spray 8 custard cups with cooking spray.

2. In a medium bowl, place the eggs, milk, and oil. Beat with an electric mixer until combined. In a small bowl, sift the flour and salt together. Add it to the eggs, and mix with the electric mixer until it is smooth. Scrape down the sides of the bowl with a rubber spatula and mix again.

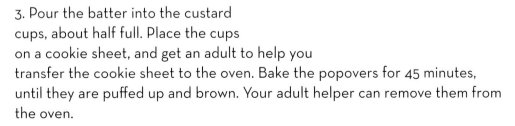

3. Pour the batter into the custard cups, about half full. Place the cups on a cookie sheet, and get an adult to help you transfer the cookie sheet to the oven. Bake the popovers for 45 minutes, until they are puffed up and brown. Your adult helper can remove them from the oven.

4. You will have to get an adult to help you take the popovers out of the hot custard cups. Running a butter knife around the edge of the cups will help loosen the popovers. Serve immediately, as they will deflate as they sit. Serve with soft butter and jelly.

Makes 8 popovers

Fruit Dip

This is great with any fruit.

Small
bowl

Dry measuring cups

Measuring
spoons

Electric
mixer

3 ounces cream cheese,
at room temperature

¼ cup confectioners'
sugar

¼ cup
sour cream

2 tablespoons
marshmallow crème

½ teaspoon
vanilla extract

½ teaspoon
almond extract

Place all ingredients in a small bowl and cream with an electric mixer until fluffy and smooth. Cover and chill. Serve with fresh fruit of your choice.

Makes about 1 cup of dip

Bacon-Cheddar Meat Loaf

Leftovers make a great sandwich the next day!

Large
skillet

Tongs

Wooden
spoon

Medium
bowl

Dry measuring cups

Measuring
spoons

9-by-5-by-3-inch
loaf pan

Oven
mitts

4 slices
bacon

1 small onion,
chopped

1½ pounds lean
ground beef

2
eggs

⅓ cup dry
bread crumbs

½ cup grated sharp
Cheddar cheese

½ teaspoon
salt

½ teaspoon
pepper

1. Position oven rack in the middle of the oven. Preheat the oven to 375 degrees.

2. In the skillet, fry the bacon until crisp. Remove bacon, and have an adult help you drain off all but about a teaspoon of fat. In the same skillet, stir-fry the onion until it is soft, about 5 minutes. Place the onion into a medium bowl, then crumble bacon and add to bowl. Add the rest of the ingredients, and stir them together with your hands or a wooden spoon until everything is well mixed.

3. Pack the meat mixture into the loaf pan and smooth off the top with the back of the spoon.

4. Bake for 1 hour. Have your adult helper remove the pan from the oven and drain off all of the fat. Let the meat loaf sit for about 10 minutes before slicing.

Makes one 9-inch loaf that can be sliced into 6 to 8 slices

Garlic Mashed Potatoes

I just gotta have a tater with my meat loaf!

Vegetable
peeler

Cutting
board

Medium, sharp
knife

Medium
pot

Measuring
spoons

Fork

Colander

Liquid
measuring cup

Potato
masher

Rubber
spatula

4 small baking
potatoes

1½ teaspoons
salt

2 cloves garlic,
minced

½ stick butter, at
room temperature,
plus additional for
serving

½ cup
half-and-half

¼ teaspoon
pepper

1. Peel the potatoes and have an adult help you quarter them. Place them in the pot and cover them with water. Add 1 teaspoon salt and the minced garlic. Bring the potatoes to a boil and then reduce the heat to medium. Boil the potatoes for about 18 to 20 minutes, until very tender when pierced with a fork.

2. Have an adult help you drain the potatoes in a colander and return them to the hot pot. Add the half stick of butter and the half-and-half. Use the potato masher to mash the potatoes. Add ½ teaspoon salt and the pepper, and stir with the spatula to get all of the potatoes from the bottom of the pot.

3. Serve warm with additional butter.

Serves 4

Snap Beans

This is the classic Southern vegetable.

Colander

Medium
pot

Measuring
spoons

Liquid
measuring cup

1½ pounds fresh
snap beans

1 teaspoon House
Seasoning (see page 124)

1 tablespoon bacon
grease (optional)

2 cups
water

1 tablespoon
butter

1. Put the beans in a colander and wash them. Then snap off the ends of each bean and place them whole in the medium pot. Add the House Seasoning, the bacon grease, if using, and the water.

2. Bring to a rolling boil, and then reduce the heat to low and put the lid on the pot. Cook the beans on low for 25 minutes. Remove the lid and add the butter.

Serves 4 to 6

Drop Biscuits

Cookie
sheet

Dry measuring cups

Medium
bowl

Liquid
measuring cup

Measuring
spoons

Fork

Tablespoon

Oven
mitts

Cooking
spray

1 cup
self-rising flour

½ cup
buttermilk

½ teaspoon
baking soda

¼ cup
canola oil

1. Position oven rack in the middle of the oven. Preheat the oven to 400 degrees. Spray a cookie sheet with cooking spray.

2. Place the flour in a medium bowl. Add the buttermilk, baking soda, and oil. Stir with a fork. Drop by tablespoons onto the prepared cookie sheet.

3. Bake for about 8 to 10 minutes, until golden brown. Have an adult help you remove biscuits from oven.

Makes 12 biscuits

Black-and-White Gooey Butter Cake

I'm known for my gooey butter cakes. They are always on the menu at The Lady and Sons. You can change the basic recipe by changing the ingredients.

9-by-13-inch
baking dish

Large
bowl

Small glass
bowl

Waxed
paper

Electric
mixer

Rubber
spatula

Measuring
spoons

Dry measuring
cups

Oven
mitts

Wire
rack

Cooking
spray

One 18¼-ounce
package chocolate
cake mix

2 sticks butter

3 eggs

8 ounces cream cheese,
at room temperature

1 teaspoon
vanilla extract

3 cups confectioners'
sugar

⅓ cup
chocolate chips

1. Position oven rack in middle of oven. Preheat the oven to 350 degrees. Spray the baking dish with cooking spray.

2. Place the cake mix in a large bowl. Put 1 stick butter in a small glass bowl, cover it with waxed paper or a paper towel, and melt the butter in the microwave on high power for 45 seconds. Add 1 egg and the melted butter to the cake mix. Beat with an electric mixer until combined, about 2 minutes. Use a rubber spatula to scrape down the sides and the bottom of the bowl to get all of the cake mix combined. The batter will be very stiff.

3. Use the rubber spatula to scrape out the batter into the baking dish. Use your clean hands to pat the batter evenly into the bottom of the dish.

4. Rinse out the large bowl and wash the beaters. Dry them. Place the cream cheese in the large bowl and beat with the electric mixer until it is smooth, about 1 minute. Add 2 eggs and the vanilla extract, and mix again for about 30 seconds. In the small glass bowl, melt the remaining stick of butter as in step 2. Add the melted butter and the confectioners' sugar to the cream cheese mixture, and mix until very smooth, about 2 minutes. Use the rubber spatula to scrape down the sides and the bottom of the bowl. Pour this mixture evenly over the chocolate layer.

5. Take the chocolate chips and sprinkle them evenly over the top of the white layer.

6. Bake for about 40 minutes, until the sides have begun to pull away from the dish and the white filling appears set. It will have a slight jiggle, but you need that for the "gooey" part. The chocolate layer will be peeking out from under the white layer, but that's okay!

7. Have an adult help you remove the dish from the oven, and let it sit on a wire rack on the counter for *at least two hours* so that the cake will set before you cut it into bars. The cake will be puffed up, then will deflate and firm up as it cools. When it is cool, cut it into 24 pieces. The ones around the edge are more cakelike, and the ones in the middle are gooey.

Makes 24 bars

Index